NEW DIRECTIONS FOR EVALUATION
A PUBLICATION OF THE AMERICAN EVALUATION ASSOCIATION

Gary T. Henry, *Georgia State University*
COEDITOR-IN-CHIEF

Jennifer C. Greene, *University of Illinois*
COEDITOR-IN-CHIEF

# Program Theory in Evaluation: Challenges and Opportunities

Patricia J. Rogers
*Royal Melbourne Institute of Technology*

Timothy A. Hacsi
*Harvard Children's Initiative*

Anthony Petrosino
*American Academy of Arts & Sciences*

Tracy A. Huebner
*WestEd*

EDITORS

Number 87, Fall 2000

JOSSEY-BASS
San Francisco

PROGRAM THEORY IN EVALUATION:
CHALLENGES AND OPPORTUNITIES
Patricia J. Rodgers, Timothy A. Hacsi, Anthony Petrosino,
Tracy A. Huebner (eds.)
New Directions for Evaluation, no. 87
*Jennifer C. Greene, Gary T. Henry*, Coeditors-in-Chief
Copyright ©2000 Jossey-Bass, a Wiley company.

Microfilm copies of issues and articles are available in 16mm and 35mm,
as well as microfiche in 105mm, through University Microfilms Inc., 300
North Zeeb Road, Ann Arbor, Michigan 48106-1346.

*New Directions for Evaluation* is indexed in Contents Pages in Education,
Higher Education Abstracts, and Sociological Abstracts.

ISSN_109-6736          ISBN_0-7879-5432-2

NEW DIRECTIONS FOR EVALUATION is part of The Jossey-Bass Education
Series and is published quarterly by Jossey-Bass Inc., Publishers, 350 Sansome Street, San Francisco, California 94104-1342.

SUBSCRIPTIONS cost $65.00 for individuals and $118.00 for institutions,
agencies, and libraries. Prices subject to change.

EDITORIAL CORRESPONDENCE should be addressed to the Editors-in-Chief,
Jennifer C. Greene, Department of Educational Psychology, University of
Illinois, 260E Education Building, 1310 South Sixth Street, Champaign,
IL 61820, or Gary T. Henry, School of Policy Studies, Georgia State Uni-
versity, P.O. Box 4039, Atlanta, GA 30302-4039.

www.josseybass.com

Printed in the United States of America on acid-free recycled paper con-
taining 100 percent recovered waste paper, of which at least 20 percent is
postconsumer waste.

NEW DIRECTIONS FOR EVALUATION

Sponsored by the American Evaluation Association

## Editorial Policy and Procedures

*New Directions for Evaluation,* a quarterly sourcebook, is an official publication of the American Evaluation Association. The journal publishes empirical, methodological, and theoretical works on all aspects of evaluation. A reflective approach to evaluation is an essential strand to be woven through every volume. The editors encourage volumes that have one of three foci: (1) craft volumes that present approaches, methods, or techniques that can be applied in evaluation practice, such as the use of templates, case studies, or survey research; (2) professional issue volumes that present issues of import for the field of evaluation, such as utilization of evaluation or locus of evaluation capacity; (3) societal issue volumes that draw out the implications of intellectual, social, or cultural developments for the field of evaluation, such as the women's movement, communitarianism, or multiculturalism. A wide range of substantive domains is appropriate for *New Directions for Evaluation;* however, the domains must be of interest to a large audience within the field of evaluation. We encourage a diversity of perspectives and experiences within each volume, as well as creative bridges between evaluation and other sectors of our collective lives.

The editors do not consider or publish unsolicited single manuscripts. Each issue of the journal is devoted to a single topic, with contributions solicited, organized, reviewed, and edited by a guest editor. Issues may take any of several forms, such as a series of related chapters, a debate, or a long article followed by brief critical commentaries. In all cases, the proposals must follow a specific format, which can be obtained from the editor-in-chief. These proposals are sent to members of the editorial board and to relevant substantive experts for peer review. The process may result in acceptance, a recommendation to revise and resubmit, or rejection. However, the editors are committed to working constructively with potential guest editors to help them develop acceptable proposals.

Jennifer C. Greene, Coeditor-in-Chief
Department of Educational Psychology
University of Illinois
260E Education Building
1310 South Sixth Street
Champaign, IL 61820
email: jcgreene@uiuc.edu

Gary T. Henry, Coeditor-in-Chief
School of Policy Studies
Georgia State University
P.O. Box 4039
Atlanta, GA 30302-4039
e-mail: gthenry@gsu.edu

# CONTENTS

# Editors' Notes

It has been more than thirty years since evaluators first underscored the advantages in making explicit and testing program theory—that is, the underlying assumptions about how a program will work to achieve intended outcomes. And it has been ten years since the last of two issues of *New Directions for Program Evaluation* (the former name of the series) was devoted to providing evaluators with some of the tools needed to carry out program theory evaluations in practice and helped refine the many conceptual and practical issues involved. Since those volumes were published, the frontiers of evaluation have expanded to meet new challenges, such as performance measurement, organizational learning, collaborative and participatory research, and meta-analysis.

In *Program Theory in Evaluation: Challenges and Opportunities*, we examine the real or potential role for program theory in these newer areas. But some thorny issues remain for evaluators implementing such evaluations, particularly in regard to causal inference. Following the Introduction, Part One includes four chapters that address some of these challenges. Despite some persistent questions, there are opportunities for program theory to help evaluators in areas such as performance measurement and meta-analysis. Part Two includes four chapters that discuss this potential. The volume's summary chapter belongs to Leonard Bickman.

In Chapter One, the editors assess the current state of program theory, drawing on their own review of the available literature. They use the review as a backdrop to discuss program theory's history, its complexity of definitions and variation in lexicon, its diversity in application, and its strengths and limitations in practice.

Some of the challenges in implementing program theory in evaluation practice are addressed in Part One. A major issue for evaluators is causal inference in program theory evaluations. In Chapter Two, Jane Davidson argues that randomization is but one of several ways that scientists acknowledge can establish causal inference and that evaluation clients often accept lesser standards of proof about causality to get the information they need. She offers that a program theory evaluation could meet the lower standards of proof required in settings that evaluators often find themselves in. In contrast, Thomas Cook argues in Chapter Three that program theory is not sufficient to establish causal inference. Rather than "falsely choosing" between randomization and program theory, the evaluator can make the optimal choice and combine both.

In addition to the complexities associated with causal inference, there are challenges in deciding what types of program theories or models to test with an evaluation. There are often a number of plausible theories about how a program works and an abundance of links to consider. In a perfect world, the evaluator would be able to study them all. But as Carol Weiss writes in Chapter Four, the evaluator has to make simplifying choices. She goes on to provide guidance for evaluators who are pondering which links in which theory they should test. In Chapter Five, Patricia Rogers shows how simple models—usually depicting causation like a chain of dominoes—may not accurately reflect how programs work. She provides examples of how evaluators have developed more realistic causal models and makes the point that complexity is not the goal, but rather useful "maps" that inform subsequent decisions.

Part Two explores the potential for program theory to make contributions in evaluation's new frontiers. The advent of meta-analysis has meant that more evaluators not only are asked to make sense of multiple evaluations but also are pressured to improve their own studies for subsequent reviews. In Chapter Six, Anthony Petrosino demonstrates how even simple program theory evaluations could be used in meta-analysis to accumulate knowledge. Generalizing from a program theory evaluation in one setting to an evaluation in the next setting is Timothy Hacsi's concern in Chapter Seven. After reviewing some basic problems in program diffusion, he shows how the subtle information generated by program theory evaluation offers an alternative to current models for replicating innovations.

Another challenge faced by evaluators is getting staff buy-in for their studies. In Chapter Eight, Tracy Huebner provides several illustrative case studies to show the *value-added* of program theory in educational evaluation. Huebner finds that the approach helped evaluators coordinate their goals with those of school staff and reduced the normal resistance that teachers and administrators often have to "yet another study," particularly one that requires them to collect the data.

Evaluators are often being asked to develop systems for monitoring performance. In Chapter Nine, Sue Funnell outlines the problems encountered in developing such systems and draws on her experience to show how program theory can help evaluators develop monitoring tools that make sense. Her matrix can be used to draw out underlying theories about why agencies or programs should succeed, to identify indicators in which measurement is needed, and to ensure that important external factors outside the boundaries of the organization are also monitored.

Finally, in Chapter Ten, Leonard Bickman summarizes these contributions and outlines a future agenda for program theory evaluation. As editor of two seminal *New Directions for Program Evaluation* volumes on program theory, Bickman has the perfect perch from which to critique the volume and offer his observations and predictions.

We believe this volume offers hope and pragmatism. Program theory can help evaluators meet some of the new challenges they face. But implementing program theory evaluation certainly offers its own challenges and quandaries. Our hope is that this *New Directions* issue not only will stimulate thinking about program theory evaluation but also—and even more important—will result in an increase in real-world tests and applications.

Anthony Petrosino
Patricia J. Rogers
Tracy A. Huebner
Timothy A. Hacsi
Editors

ANTHONY PETROSINO *is research fellow at the Center for Evaluation, Initiatives for Children Program, American Academy of Arts and Sciences, and research associate at the Harvard Graduate School of Education.*

PATRICIA J. ROGERS *is director of the Program for Public Sector Evaluation in the Faculty of Applied Science, Royal Melbourne Institute of Technology, Australia.*

TRACY A. HUEBNER *is coordinator for comprehensive school reform at WestEd.*

TIMOTHY A. HACSI *is research fellow at the Harvard Children's Initiative and teaches history at the Harvard Extension School.*

**1**

*The historical development of program theory evaluation,
current variations in theory and practice, and pressing
issues are discussed.*

# Program Theory Evaluation: Practice, Promise, and Problems

*Patricia J. Rogers, Anthony Petrosino, Tracy A. Huebner,
Timothy A. Hacsi*

For over thirty years now, many evaluators have recommended making explicit the underlying assumptions about how programs are expected to work—the *program theory*—and then using this theory to guide the evaluation. In this chapter, we provide an overview of *program theory evaluation* (PTE), based on our search to find what was *value-added* to evaluations that used this approach. We found fewer clear-cut, full-blown examples in practice than expected, but we found many interesting variations of PTE in practice and much to recommend it. And elements of PTE, whether the evaluators use the terminology or not, are being used in a wide range of areas of concern to evaluators. Based on this review, in this chapter we discuss the practice, promise, and problems of PTE.

## What Is Program Theory Evaluation?

Because this volume is intended to demonstrate the diversity of practice, we have used a broad definition of program theory evaluation. We consider it to have two essential components, one conceptual and one empirical. PTE consists of an explicit theory or model of how the program causes the intended or observed outcomes and an evaluation that is at least partly guided by this model. This definition, though deliberately broad, does exclude some versions of evaluation that have the word *theory* attached to them. It does not cover all six types of theory-driven evaluation defined by Chen (1990) but only the type he refers to as *intervening mechanism evaluation*. It does not include evaluations that explicate the theory behind a

New Directions for Evaluation, no. 87, Fall 2000 © Jossey-Bass program but that do not use the theory to guide the evaluation. Nor does it include evaluations in which the program theory is a list of activities, like a "to do" list, rather than a model showing a series of intermediate outcomes, or mechanisms, by which the program activities are understood to lead to the desired ends.

The idea of basing program evaluation on a causal model of the program is not a new one. At least as far back as the 1960s, Suchman suggested that program evaluation might address the achievement of a "chain of objectives" (1967, p. 55) and argued for the benefit of doing this. "The evaluation study tests some hypothesis that activity A will attain objective B because it is able to influence process C which affects the occurrence of this objective, An understanding of all three factors—program, objective and intervening process—is essential to the conduct of evaluative research" (1967, p. 177).

Weiss (1972) went on to explain how an evaluation could identify several possible causal models of a teacher home-visiting program and could determine which was the best as supported by evidence. In the three decades since, many different terms have been used for this type of evaluation, including *outcomes hierarchies* (Bennett, 1975) and *theory-of-action* (Schön, 1997). More commonly, the terms *program theory* (Bickman, 1987, 1990), *theory-based evaluation* (Weiss, 1995, 1997), and *program logic* (Lenne and Cleland, 1987; Funnell, 1997) have been used.

Unfortunately, although there are clear variations in types of PTE, these different labels have not been used consistently to refer to different types and have instead tended to reflect the preferred label in a particular organization or source references. Even though this volume uses the term program theory evaluation in its title, some of the authors use other terms.

Interest in program theory has grown significantly since two previous *New Directions* volumes on the topic (Bickman, 1987, 1990). More agencies and organizations, both in the United States and abroad, are at least paying lip service to program theory. Federal research funders such as the National Institutes of Health now require discussions of program theory in applications submitted for evaluation support. Many not-for-profit agencies have followed the United Way's lead in developing performance mesures based on a generic causal model of inputs-processes-outputs-outcomes (Hatry, van Houten, Plantz, and Greenway, 1996). Arguments for including program theory in evaluation are now appearing not only in evaluation journals but also in discipline-specific journals, such as those in education, criminology, and sociology. The largest-selling evaluation textbook, *Program Evaluation: A Systematic Approach,* has now, in its sixth edition, added a chapter on this approach (Rossi, Freeman, and Lipsey, 1999). Similarly, *Evaluation Models: Evaluation of Educational and Social Programs* (Madaus, Stufflebeam, and Scriven, 1983) has added a chapter on program theory evaluation in its second edition (Rogers, forthcoming).

## Practice: Diverse Choices to Meet Diverse Needs

Program theory is know by many different names, created in many different ways, and used for any number of purposes. Here we provide a brief road map to the variety of ways people think about and employ program theory.

**Locating Examples.**   To try to understand the variety of ways in which program theory evaluation is now being used, we began in early 1998 to comb through available bibliographical databases, citation indexes, and evaluation reports. We also reviewed conference proceedings, dissertations, and articles from a variety of disciplines. In addition, we received many helpful examples in response to an inquiry to the American Evaluation Association's Internet discussion list, EVALTALK. Our efforts turned up examples dating from 1957 to 2000 from the United States, Canada, Australia, New Zealand, and the United Kingdom. We have not included every example that we located in this volume but instead have used examples to identify and illustrate critical challenges in using program theory or ways of addressing them.

Our review showed amazing diversity in theory and practice across two main areas—how program theories are developed and how they are used to guide evaluations.

**Developing the Program Theory—Who, When, and What.**   In some evaluations, the program theory has been developed largely by the evaluator, based on a review of research literature on similar programs or relevant causal mechanisms, through discussions with key informants, through a review of program documentation, or through observation of the program itself (Lipsey and Pollard, 1989). In other evaluations, the program theory has been developed primarily by those associated with the program, often through a group process. Many practitioners advise using a combination of these approaches (Pawson and Tilley, 1995; Patton, 1996; see also Funnell, Chapter Nine).

The program theory can be developed before the program is implemented or after the program is under way. At times, it is used to change program practice as the evaluation is beginning. Most program theories are summarized in a diagram showing a causal chain. Among the many variations, we will highlight just three for now; Rogers discusses other variations in Chapter Five.

At its simplest, a program theory shows a single intermediate outcome by which the program achieves its ultimate outcome. For example, in a program designed to reduce substance abuse, we might test whether or not the program succeeds in changing knowledge about possible dangers and then whether or not this seems important in achieving the desired behavior change. As Petrosino (Chapter Six) points out, for some program areas, articulating this mediating variable and measuring it would be a significant advance on current practice.

More complex program theories show a series of intermediate outcomes, sometimes in multiple strands that combine to cause the ultimate outcomes. So for a substance abuse prevention program, we might theorize that an effective program will generate a positive reaction among participants, change both attitudes and knowledge, and develop participants' skills in resisting peer pressure. Although these more complex program theories may more adequately represent the complexity of programs, it is impossible to design an evaluation that adequately covers all the factors they identify. Weiss (Chapter Four) proposes some ways to select the particular causal links that any one evaluation might study.

The third type of program theory is represented by a series of boxes labeled *inputs, processes, outputs,* and *outcomes,* with arrows connecting them. It is not specified which processes lead to which outputs. Instead the different components of a program theory are simply listed in each box. Although this type of program theory does not show the relationships among different components, these relationships are sometimes explored in the empirical component of the evaluation.

**Using the Program Theory to Guide the Evaluation.**    Program theory has been used in quite different ways to guide evaluation. Examples show diversity in the purpose and audience of the evaluation, the type of research design, and the type of data collected. Within this diversity, it is possible to identify two broad clusters of practice.

In some PTEs, the main purpose of the evaluation is to test the program theory, to identify what it is about the program that causes the outcomes. This sort of PTE is most commonly used in large, well-resourced evaluations focused on such summative questions as, Does this program work? and Should this pilot be extended? These theory-testing PTEs wrestle with the issue of causal attribution—sometimes using experimental or quasi-experimental designs in conjunction with program theory and sometimes using program theory as an alternative to these designs. Such evaluations can be particularly helpful in distinguishing between theory failure and implementation failure (Lipsey, 1993; Weiss, 1997). By identifying and measuring the intermediate steps of program implementation and the initial impacts, we can begin to answer these questions. These intermediate outcomes also provide some interim measure of program success for programs with long-term intended outcomes.

An example of this type of program theory evaluation can be found in the Family Empowerment Project evaluation, in which Bickman and colleagues (1998) conducted an experimental test of the effects of a program that trained parents to be stronger advocates for children in the mental health system. They articulated a model of how the program was assumed to work. First, parent training would increase the parent's knowledge, self-efficacy, and advocacy skills. Second, parents would then become more involved in their child's mental health care. Finally, this collaboration would lead to the child's improved mental health outcomes.

But they did not stop with the articulation of a program theory. They also constructed measures, collected data, and analyzed them to test these underlying assumptions. The program was able to achieve statistically significant effects on parental knowledge and self-efficacy, but no useful measures for testing advocacy skills could be found. Unfortunately, the intervention had no apparent effect on caregiver involvement in treatment or service use and ultimately had no impact on the eventual mental health status of the children.

Evaluations such as these seem to be at least implicitly based on Weiss's definition of program theory, "[It] refers to the *mechanisms* that mediate between the delivery (and receipt) of the program and the emergence of the outcomes of interest" (1998, p. 57).

The other type of program theory evaluation is often seen in small evaluations done at the project level by or on behalf of project managers and staff. In these cases, program theory is more likely to be used for formative evaluation, to guide their daily actions and decisions, than for summative evaluation. Such PTEs are often not concerned with causal attribution. Although some of these evaluations pay attention to the influence of external factors, there is rarely systematic ruling out of rival explanations for the outcomes. Many of these evaluations have been developed in response to the increasing demands for programs and agencies to report performance information and to demonstrate their use of evaluation to improve their services. In these circumstances, PTE has often been highly regarded because of the benefits it provides to program managers and staff in terms of improved planning and management, in addition to its use as an evaluation tool.

Stewart, Cotton, Duckett, and Meleady (1990) provide an example of this type of PTE in their evaluation of a project that recruited and trained volunteers to provide emotional support for people with AIDS, their lovers, families, and friends. The paper did not provide a diagram of the program theory model nor present any data. Instead Stewart and colleagues reported on the process of developing the model, the types of data that were gathered, and how the data were used. "Performance indicators developed by Ankali [the project] were both for the organisation's own purposes and to meet the requirements of the funding body. Both qualitative and quantitative indicators were selected. . . . Ankali now uses the outcomes hierarchy during orientation of volunteers and report[s] that the process has assisted with improved targeting of volunteers and referral agencies, modification to the training program, supervision of clients and volunteers, and development of proposals for expansion and enhancement of the service" (1990, p. 317).

This type of program theory evaluation appears to be closer to that described by Wholey. "[It] identifies program resources, program activities, and intended program outcomes, and specifies a chain of causal assumptions linking program resources, activities, intermediate outcomes and ultimate program goals" (1987, p. 78).

Despite the apparent popularity of program theory evaluation, we found that the formal evaluation literature still has comparatively few examples. For instance, when we searched the abstracts in six bibliographical databases for the time frame 1995–1999, we found program theory explicitly mentioned in evaluations of children's programs only twice. In addition, many of the evaluations that we found used theory in very limited and specific ways, for example, to help plan an evaluation, but very few used theory as extensively as the most prominent proponents of this approach suggest. But PTEs conducted in small projects or local sites are rarely published in refereed journals or distributed widely, being more likely to be presented as conference papers by practitioners or presented in performance measurement forums. And many of them fail to include what some would consider an essential component of a program theory evaluation—systematic testing of the causal model.

In this volume, we include examples of both types of PTE. Weiss (Chapter Four), Hacsi (Chapter Seven), and Petrosino (Chapter Six) discuss issues associated with *theory-testing PTEs*. Huebner (Chapter Eight) discusses four examples of *action-guiding PTEs*, and Funnell (Chapter Nine) discusses a technique for assisting with this sort of PTE.

## Promises and Problems

Program theory has been seen as an answer to many different problems in evaluation. Here we briefly discuss several areas where program theory has been seen as promising.

**Understanding Why Programs Do or Do Not Work.**    Among the promises made for PTE, the most tantalizing is that it provides some clues to answer the question of why programs work or fail to work. Consider the usual practice of trying to understand why a program succeeded or failed. Following reporting of results, evaluators usually work in a post hoc manner to suggest reasons for observed results (Petrosino, forthcoming, 2000). But without data, such post hoc theories are never tested, and given the poor state of replication in the social sciences, they are likely never to be.

In contrast, by creating a model of the microsteps or linkages in the causal path from program to ultimate outcome—and empirically testing it—PTE provides something more about why the program failed or succeeded in reaching the distal goals it had hoped to achieve, as in Bickman and colleagues' evaluation of the family empowerment program (1998). Perhaps the intervention was not able to improve advocacy skills—remember, those could not be measured. Or maybe there was a critical mechanism missing from the model, which the program was not activating or engaging. We learn something more than the program's apparent lack of impact on children's mental health.

Even if all these issues cannot be adequately addressed in the original evaluation, a PTE can provide an agenda for the next program and evaluation.

For example, a critical link in the Bickman and colleagues study was not tested (advocacy skills acquisition), given the paucity of measurement development in this area. Pointing out this deficiency suggests an agenda to develop an instrument to measure this variable in the next similar study.

**Attributing Outcomes to the Program.**    Another promise sometimes made for PTE is better evidence for causal attribution—to answer the question of whether the program caused the observed outcomes. Program theory has been used by evaluators to develop better evidence for attributing outcomes to a program in circumstances where random assignment is not possible (for example, Homel, 1990, in an evaluation of random breath testing of automobile drivers). In the absence of a counterfactual, support for causal attribution can come from evidence of achievement of intermediate outcomes, investigation of alternative explanations for outcomes, and pattern matching. Support for causal attribution can also come from program stakeholder assessments (for example, Funnell and Mograby, 1995, in their evaluation of the impact of program evaluations in a road and traffic authority) or from data about a range of indicators, including data on external factors likely to influence the theorized causal pathway (for example, Ward, Maine, McCarthy, and Kamara, 1994, in their evaluation of activities to reduce maternal mortality in developing countries). It may be possible to develop testable hypotheses on the basis of the causal model (Pawson and Tilley, 1995), especially if the model includes contingencies or differentiation—expected differences in outcomes depending on differences in context. Causal attribution is also sometimes addressed by combining traditional experimental or quasi-experimental designs with PTE.

Many PTEs do not address attribution at all, simply reporting implementation of activities and achievement of intended outcomes. This approach is particularly common where program theory is used to develop ongoing monitoring and performance information systems. Causal attribution in PTEs is discussed in more detail in the chapters in this volume by Cook (Chapter Three), Davidson (Chapter Two), and Hacsi (Chapter Seven).

**Improving the Program.**    Many of the claims for the benefits of PTE refer to its capacity to improve programs directly and indirectly. Articulating a program theory can expose faulty thinking about why the program should work, which can be corrected before things are up and running at full speed (Weiss, 1995). The process of developing a program theory can itself be a rewarding experience, as staff develop common understanding of their work and identify the most important components. Many accounts of PTE (such as Milne, 1993; and Huebner, Chapter Eight) report that this has been the most positive benefit from conducting PTE. In this way, PTE is very similar to the earlier technique of evaluability assessment.

But PTE is supposed to then use the program theory to guide the evaluation, and it is here that some evaluations falter. Whereas collaboratively building a program theory can be an energizing team activity, exposing this to harsh empirical tests can be less attractive. Practical difficulties abound as well. When PTE is implemented at a small project, staff may not have the time or skills to collect and analyze data in ways that either test the program theory or provide useful information to guide decisions and action. If program theory is used to develop accountability systems, there is a real risk of *goal displacement,* wherein staff seek to achieve targets and stated objectives at the cost of achieving the ultimate goal or sustainability of the program (Winston, 1991).

## Conclusion

In this chapter, we have outlined the range of activity that can be considered program theory evaluation and have identified major issues in its theory and practice. These are discussed in more detail by the other chapters in this volume.

## References

Bennett, C. "Up the Hierarchy." *Journal of Extension,* 1975, *13*(2), 7–12.

Bickman, L. (ed.). *Using Program Theory in Evaluation.* New Directions for Program Evaluation, no. 33. San Francisco: Jossey-Bass, 1987.

Bickman, L. (ed.). *Advances in Program Theory.* New Directions for Program Evaluation, no. 47. San Francisco: Jossey-Bass, 1990.

Bickman, L., and others. "Long-Term Outcomes to Family Caregiver Empowerment." *Journal of Child and Family Studies,* 1998, 7(3), 269–282.

Chen, H. T. *Theory-Driven Evaluation.* Thousand Oaks, Calif.: Sage, 1990.

Funnell, S. "Program Logic: An Adaptable Tool." *Evaluation News and Comment,* 1997, 6(1), 5–17.

Funnell, S., and Mograby, A. "Evaluating Employment Programs Delivered by Community Organisations." *Proceedings of the Annual Conference of the Australasian Evaluation Society,* 1995, 2, 531–552.

Hatry, H., van Houten, T., Plantz, M. C., and Greenway, M. T. *Measuring Program Outcomes: A Practical Approach.* Alexandria, Va.: United Way of America, 1996.

Homel, R. "Random Breath Testing in New South Wales: The Evaluation of a Successful Social Experiment." *National Evaluation Conference 1990, Proceedings,* vol. 1. Australasian Evaluation Society, 1990.

Lenne, B., and Cleland, H. "Describing Program Logic." *Program Evaluation Bulletin 1987,* no. 2. Public Service Board of New South Wales, 1987.

Lipsey, M. W. "Theory as Method: Small Theories of Treatments." In L. Sechrest and A. Scott (eds.), *Understanding Causes and Generalizing About Them.* New Directions for Program Evaluation, no. 57. San Francisco: Jossey-Bass, 1993.

Lipsey, M. W., and Pollard, J. "Driving Toward Theory in Program Evaluation: More Models to Choose From." *Evaluation and Program Planning,* 1989, *12*, 317–328.

Madaus, G., Stufflebeam, D., and Scriven, M. *Evaluation Models: Evaluation of Educational and Social Programs.* Norwell, Mass.: Kluwer, 1983.

Milne, C. "Outcomes Hierarchies and Program Logic as Conceptual Tools: Five Case Studies." Paper presented at the international conference of the Australasian Evaluation Society, Brisbane, 1993.

Patton, M. Q. *Utilization-Focused Evaluation.* (3rd ed.) Thousand Oaks, Calif.: Sage, 1996.

Pawson, R., and Tilley, N. *Realistic Evaluation.* London: Sage, 1995.

Petrosino, A. J. "Answering the Why Question in Evaluation: The Causal-Model Approach." *Canadian Journal of Program Evaluation,* 2000, *15*(1), 1–24.

Rogers, P. J. "Program Theory Evaluation: Not Whether Programs Work But Why." In G. Madaus, D. Stufflebeam, and T. Kelleher (eds.), *Evaluation Models: Evaluation of Educational and Social Programs.* Norwell, Mass.: Kluwer, forthcoming.

Rossi, P. H., Freeman, H., and Lipsey, M. W. *Program Evaluation: A Systematic Approach.* Thousand Oaks, Calif.: Sage, 1999.

Schön, D. A. "Theory-of-Action Evaluation." Paper presented to the Harvard Evaluation Task Force, Apr. 1997.

Stewart, K., Cotton, R., Duckett, M., and Meleady, K. "The New South Wales Program Logic Model: The Experience of the AIDS Bureau, New South Wales Department of Health." *Proceedings of the Annual Conference of the Australasian Evaluation Society,* 1990, *2,* 315–322.

Suchman, E. A. *Evaluative Research: Principles and Practice in Public Service and Social Action Programs.* New York: Russell Sage Foundation, 1967.

Ward, V. M., Maine, D., McCarthy, J., and Kamara, A. "A Strategy for the Evaluation of Activities to Reduce Mortality in Developing Countries." *Evaluation Review,* 1994, *18,* 438–457.

Weiss, C. H. *Evaluation Research: Methods of Assessing Program Effectiveness.* Englewood Cliffs, N.J.: Prentice Hall, 1972.

Weiss, C. H. "Nothing As Practical As Good Theory: Exploring Theory-Based Evaluation for Comprehensive Community Initiatives for Children and Families." In J. P. Connell, A. C. Kubisch, L. B. Schorr, and C. H. Weiss (eds.), *New Approaches to Evaluating Community Initiatives: Concepts, Methods and Contexts.* Washington, D.C.: Aspen Institute, 1995.

Weiss, C. H. "How Can Theory-Based Evaluation Make Greater Headway?" *Evaluation Review,* 1997, *21,* 501–524.

Weiss, C. H. *Evaluation: Methods for Studying Programs and Policies.* (2nd ed.) Englewood Cliffs, N.J.: Prentice Hall, 1998.

Wholey, J. S. "Evaluability Assessment: Developing Program Theory." In L. Bickman (ed.), *Using Program Theory in Evaluation.* New Directions for Program Evaluation, no. 33. San Francisco: Jossey-Bass, 1987.

Winston, J. A. "Linking Evaluation and Performance Management." Paper presented at the annual conference of the Australasian Evaluation Society, Adelaide, 1991.

*PATRICIA J. ROGERS is director of the Program for Public Sector Evaluation in the Faculty of Applied Science, Royal Melbourne Institute of Technology, Australia.*

*ANTHONY PETROSINO is research fellow at the Center for Evaluation, Initiatives for Children Program, American Academy of Arts and Sciences, and research associate at the Harvard Graduate School of Education.*

*TRACY A. HUEBNER is coordinator for comprehensive school reform at WestEd.*

*TIMOTHY A. HACSI is research fellow at the Harvard Children's Initiative and teaches history at the Harvard Extension School.*

# PART ONE

## Challenges In Practice

**2**

*This chapter explores the relative strengths and weaknesses of program theory as a tool for inferring causality and outlines a five-stage approach that makes increased use of inductively built program theories and takes more deliberate account of the varying levels of certainty that are required for evaluative conclusions.*

# Ascertaining Causality in Theory-Based Evaluation

*E. Jane Davidson*

"Causation. The relation between mosquitos and mosquito bites" (Scriven, 1991, p. 77). Although causality is easily understood in everyday life, formulating a precise definition that spells out how it must be demonstrated proves to be considerably more difficult (for example, Sosa and Tooley, 1993). Rather than delving into this difficult philosophical debate, this chapter focuses on the main issue for the practicing evaluator—determining whether observed changes are due to the program (and can correctly be referred to as program effects), are due to some other cause, or are purely coincidental.

Why is causality important? If an evaluator erroneously concludes that a program is meritorious (because it is thought to have caused some positive changes), resources may be wasted on continuing it or expanding it in its current form. In addition to the obvious monetary costs to funders, there are serious opportunity costs for recipients and program staff, who could be putting their time and efforts into something more worthwhile. Conversely, a good program might be discontinued or altered if negative changes are wrongly attributed to it or if its positive effects are thought to be due to something else. In other words, causality is not merely an issue of relevance to academics; it deeply affects the lives of many stakeholder groups, whether they realize it or not.

The attribution of causality to programs and other types of evaluand is a daunting challenge. However, there are a number of methods available, both traditional and nontraditional, that can help the practitioner address this issue. This chapter explores the relative strengths and weaknesses of program theory as a tool for inferring causality and makes two broad recommendations: pay greater attention to the decision-making context, and increase the use of inductively built program theories. A set of criteria for inferring causality is outlined, as is a step-by-step strategy intended to guide the practitioner through the process of building an evidence base for causal attributions.

There are a number of terms currently in use that describe the kind of evaluation first proposed by Suchman (1967) and later developed by Weiss (1972), Bickman (1987), Chen (1990), Lipsey (1993), and others. In this chapter, I have used the term *theory-based* rather than *theory-driven* in order to avoid the impression that any particular theory should "drive" the evaluation. I have also avoided the term *program theory evaluation* because it could be construed to imply that the main task is the evaluation of program theory rather than the evaluation of the program itself. As some examples in the next section illustrate, these definitional issues are far more important than they first appear because they may lean the evaluator toward approaches to using program theory that limit his or her ability to infer causality. In this chapter, the term *theory-based evaluation* refers to the use of program theory (or *logic models*) as a framework in the determination of merit or worth.

## Testing Causal Mechanisms with Theory-Based Evaluation

The introduction and development of theory-based evaluation and its variants (for example, Bickman, 1987; Chen, 1990; Lipsey, 1993; Suchman, 1967; Weiss, 1972) sparked an increased focus on understanding the mechanisms by which programs produce their effects. This is an important development because we can increase our confidence in a causal claim if we have some understanding of the causal mechanism involved (Sayer, 1992). A claim such as "drug resistance education programs cause increased drug use" becomes considerably more convincing when at least one element in the causal chain is illuminated. For example, Donaldson, Graham, and Hansen (1994) discovered that students who received such a program not only reported higher levels of drug use in later years but also considered drug use in school to be significantly more prevalent than those who had not taken the resistance program. When the links between these elements were tested and found to be significant, the evidence in favor of a causal effect was enhanced still further.

Despite the purported focus of theory-based evaluation on investigating the causal mechanisms by which a program achieves its effects, surprisingly few actually do this. For example, Weiss (1997) inspected some thirty studies that claimed to draw on program theory and found that very few of them measured the mediator variables identified in the model, let alone tested the links between them and the program and its outcomes. However, logic models are often used in other ways.

Many evaluations appear to use program theory as a framework for determining the variables that should be measured in an evaluation or as a means of better understanding the evaluand. For example, an evaluation of Project TEAMS (Technology Enhancing Achievement in Middle School), meta-evaluated by Cooksy (1999), used a logic model to provide a conceptual representation of the program, of which a small fraction of the variables were measured (often necessary when there are budgetary constraints). The model provided a useful conceptualization of the program, although the causal links specified in the model were not tested. Accordingly, Cooksy noted that one of the major weaknesses of the evaluation was "the inability to attribute the changes reported to TEAMS" (p. 135).

Saxe and Tighe's (1999) evaluation of Fighting Back, a series of community programs designed to combat alcohol and drug use, encountered a similar problem. The authors used a very comprehensive logic model to identify a wide range of important variables that were measured as part of the evaluation, thereby ensuring good coverage of key performance criteria. However, Saxe and Tighe also reported difficulty inferring causality, attributing this to their inability to use randomized designs and the unavailability of control groups.

In both of the preceding cases, the evaluators appear to have been constrained in their ability to employ more complex experimental or quasi-experimental designs (Cook and Campbell, 1979), a factor that no doubt contributed to their problems with the causality issue. But how might it have helped to test the linkages among the variables in the program models, and what could they have concluded from such tests?

Reynolds's evaluation (1998) of the High/Scope Perry Preschool Program for disadvantaged children not only specified a comprehensive logic model for the evaluand but also tested the links in the model using structural equation modeling. When testing the causal mechanism, expected changes in the mediators and outcome variables, coupled with a good fit of the data to the hypothesized model, were considered to be strong evidence that the program was indeed causing the effects. However, as Reynolds noted, "Inferences about treatment are largely dependent on the validity of the program theory" (p. 217).

Reynolds's comment hits squarely on the greatest weakness of the theory-testing approach to the use of logic models in evaluation. Even when the model appears to be strongly supported, the fact remains that any number of models might fit the data, making it impossible to conclude that a model is "correct" simply because it "fits" (Cohen and Cohen, 1983).

If alternative logic models are developed exclusively from existing theory or stakeholder input, or both, as recommended by Chen (1990), the possibility remains that one or more important causal chains (or alternative explanations) exist that are not covered by existing theory or did not occur to either stakeholders or evaluators. This may not be fatal in an evaluation whose primary purpose is to build organizational capacity for self-evaluation and inquiry or in instances where other evidence already provides the required level of certainty about causal attributions. However, failing to check a possible causal chain may be a serious flaw in a high-stakes evaluation, when accurate causal inference is critical to being able to draw defensible conclusions.

## Hunting for Causal Mechanisms

The difficulty associated with tracking down potential causes is very similar to that of hunting for side effects. Most evaluators who use program theory would agree that unintended consequences are just as important to track down as goal-related outcomes (for example, Chen, 1990). However, a program model that is generated from program goals (or theory derived from the academic literature or from stakeholders) inevitably focuses primarily on intended outcomes and is therefore in considerable danger of failing to include important potential side effects as variables in the model (Rogers and McDonald, 1999).

The same will be true in the hunt for causal explanations using these theories. A causal model built using social science or stakeholder theory, or both, may fail to include not only potential side effects (and the causal chains leading to them) but also any causal paths not predicted by the program theory.

There has been considerable work in the development of qualitative methods that trace causal chains of events to produce defensible conclusions. Examples include the *modus operandi method* used by detectives to investigate crime (Scriven, 1974a), *process tracing* (Ford and others, 1989), and *qualitative causal modeling* (Miles and Huberman, 1994). Because these methods have strong similarities, it would be redundant to discuss each one separately. Scriven's (1974a) modus operandi method provides the best *conceptual* description of the logic behind these methods and will be outlined in more detail here.

The modus operandi method uses the detective metaphor to describe the way in which potential causal explanations are identified and tested. Scriven describes how chains of causal events often leave signature "traces" that the evaluator tracks down by moving both up and down the causal chain. Starting with the observed effects (the "clues"), one can move up the causal chain, identifying what might have caused them. Using the previous example of the drug resistance training program (Donaldson, Graham, and Hansen, 1994), one could start with the increase in self-reported student drug use and search for possible reasons—for example, by asking students what they think gave rise to the increase or by observing their behavior.

In the opposite direction, one can start with the program itself (the "suspect") and trace down the causal chain to see what impacts it might have had, and through what mechanisms. If evidence is consistent with the expected trace left by a particular causal chain, then confidence in that chain as the correct causal explanation is increased. Evidence that contradicts the expected trace eliminates that causal chain as a possibility, and missing evidence makes the explanation more doubtful. In the Donaldson, Graham, and Hansen (1994) study, the increased prevalence estimates support the explanation that the program increased self-reported drug use by making students think drug use was more widespread than they had previously believed. Had prevalence estimates not increased, that causal chain would have been eliminated as a possibility.

## Methods of Inferring Causality

Scriven (1974a) describes two methods for inferring causality using the modus operandi method. The first is *causal list inference:* suppose we have a list of almost all possible causes of a certain effect. If the effect occurred, and only one of the possible causes occurred, then it is very probable that that was the true cause. The second is *modus operandi inference:* if more than one of the possible causes occurred, but only the characteristic causal chain (or modus operandi) for one of those possible causes was present, then that was probably the cause, especially if the modus operandi is highly distinctive.

What other criteria might the evaluator use to help build an evidence base for causal inference? The three most commonly used criteria are those proposed by philosopher David Hume (as cited in Huberman and Miles, 1998). They are *temporal precedence* (A before B), *constant conjunction* (when A, always B), and *contiguity of influence* (a plausible mechanism links A and B). Unfortunately, there are problems with some of these criteria if taken too literally. For example, the constant conjunction criterion might imply that a program should have similar impacts on every type of recipient in every context, and the contiguity of influence criterion might lead one to discount mechanisms that seem implausible because they are not well known. However, all are still useful rules of thumb for checking causal claims, as long as they are not applied too rigidly.

Huberman and Miles (1998) suggest four additional criteria taken from the field of epidemiology. They are *strength of association* (much more B with A than with other possible causes), *biological gradient* (if more A, then more B), *coherence* (the A-B relationship fits with what else we know about A and B), and *analogy* (A and B resemble the well-established pattern noted in C and D). Although not all of these criteria would fit every possible evaluation situation, and they could not alone constitute sufficient evidence to infer causality, they clearly add some useful sources of evidence that could be used by evaluators with access to either qualitative or quantitative data. The following is a list of the *nine potential types of evidence for inferring causality:*

1.  Causal list inference (almost all Bs are caused by A, A', A", . . ., or $A_n$; B has occurred; A did occur; but A', A", . . ., $A_n$ did not occur).

2. Modus operandi inference—use if more than one possible cause occurred (only the characteristic causal chain/modus operandi for one of the possible causes, A, was present; inference strengthened if the modus operandi in question is highly distinctive).
3. Temporal precedence (A before B).
4. Constant conjunction (when A, always B).
5. Contiguity of influence (a plausible mechanism links A and B).
6. Strength of association (much more B with A than with other possible causes).
7. Biological gradient (if more A, then more B).
8. Coherence (the A-B relationship fits with what else we know about A and B).
9. Analogy (A and B resemble the well-established pattern noted in C and D).

## Causal Tracing: A Five-Stage Process

The nine potential types of evidence for inferring causality provide a useful starting point for the practitioner attempting to develop a body of evidence that either confirms or refutes whether a program did in fact give rise to observed changes. But how can the practitioner maximize the power of theory-based evaluation to build an evidence base for causal attribution, given the problems highlighted earlier with the traditional theory-testing approach?

Two changes to the way we use theory-based evaluation should help alleviate these problems. The first is gaining a solid understanding of the decision-making context, as well as the information needs of the client. The second is supplementing tests of program theory with a more open-ended causal tracing and inductive approach to theory building, an approach referred to here as *goal-free theory-based evaluation*. To illustrate these recommendations and guide the practitioner, I would like to propose a *five-stage process for causal tracing using theory-based evaluation*.

1. Information needs assessment, which determines required level of certainty
2. Goal-free search for all important changes
3. Inductive hunt for the causes of those changes =, which builds draft logic model, possibly using input from program staff in the later stages
4. Supplementation of inductive program theory with additions of possible effects and causal chains from the literature
5. Test of the revised logic model, preferably using information sources and recipients not used to build the inductive model

In order to conclusively demonstrate causality in a particular case, one would have to eliminate all other possible causal explanations, including those whose mechanisms are not yet understood. In reality, 100 percent certainty is an unachievable (not to mention unnecessary) goal. As in a criminal or civil trial, the evidence needs to be sufficiently compelling to satisfy the relevant standards of proof in that context (for example, *beyond a reasonable doubt* or *preponderance of the evidence*). Similarly, in evaluation it is necessary to produce a body of evidence that will stand up to the scrutiny to which it will be subjected and that is commensurate with the relative costs of Type I errors (in causality terms, erroneously attributing a coincidental charge to a program) and Type II errors (erroneously concluding that an effect caused by the program was coincidental) in the given context. Accordingly, *stage one* in the causal tracing process involves an information needs assessment, in order to establish the degree of certainty to which conclusions about causality must be drawn. This should preferably be addressed when assessing program evaluability—that is, what information is needed, to what degree of certainty, and within what time and budgetary constraints? Note that it is not simply a matter of asking clients what they *think* is needed. Rather it is up to evaluators to determine this, based on multiple sources of information, using their evaluation expertise.

Bearing in mind the standard of proof needed for a particular evaluation, *stage two* begins with an open-ended and goal-free effort to detect all important outcomes of positive or negative value (Scriven, 1974b). Ideally, this should be carried out by someone thoroughly trained in the discipline of evaluation, but with minimal substantive knowledge of the particular type of evaluand and no knowledge of the program's specific goals. This ensures that the search does not focus primarily on outcomes that would have been predicted by theory or that were intended by staff, thereby reducing the chance that something important will be missed. The scope of this task will be dictated by the time and budgetary constraints associated with the evaluation, so it need not necessarily be hugely time consuming.

*Stage three* involves the goal-free theory-based approach—the use of inductive techniques to trace the causes of the effects uncovered in stage one. Here it would be ideal to use an individual or team that was highly skilled in the qualitative methods described earlier, with at least one member who had little knowledge of academic theories pertaining to the evaluand. At this point, the evaluation may start to incorporate the implicit theories held by program recipients or staff. However, it is not necessary (and may not be desirable) to fully involve them in the theory development process unless there are compelling reasons for doing so (for example, a lack of buy-in for evaluation results could cause serious problems in trying to implement improvements). For the evaluator on a limited budget and a tight time line, this step may involve some extended questioning of program recipients about what they attribute certain changes to. For a high-stakes evaluation, the approach will need to be considerably more thorough. In each case, the depth and breadth of the hunt for causes will need to match the required standards of proof established in stage one.

By the end of stage three, there should be a draft program theory created through a fully inductive process. This is developed further in *stage four* to incorporate any relevant theories from the literature that might shed light on missing links or puzzling data and that might identify new mechanisms that could explain the observed results. Although a comprehensive literature review would be ideal for the large-scale evaluation, the evaluator on a tight budget may find that perusal of the draft logic model by a subject matter expert would be sufficient. Program goals may also be incorporated at this point to make sure that the evaluation covers all the information the client needs.

In *stage five,* the model is tested using a combination of qualitative and quantitative methods. The focus here should be not so much on the overall statistical fit of the model, but on the testing and elimination of alternative causal explanations for the observed effects, using both qualitative and quantitative methods. This should continue until there is a sufficient body of evidence to satisfy the appropriate standards of proof for the given situation. For the evaluator on a shoestring budget, this may involve some observation or interviewing to test any potentially suspect causal paths.

## Conclusions

This chapter has noted some of the difficulties associated with the attribution of causality to programs and other types of evaluand and the strengths and limitations of theory-based evaluation as a tool for doing so. The main weakness of theory-based evaluation in this respect was its overreliance on the validity of a program theory that rested on prior knowledge, either from the social science literature or from program staff.

The hunt for alternative causal explanations in addition to predicted explanations is as important and as difficult as the hunt for side effects in addition to intended outcomes. Missing just one serious alternative could spell the difference between a valid and an invalid conclusion, and there are no predetermined road maps for ensuring that all possibilities have been covered. In an attempt to guide the practitioner through this challenging task, a five-stage strategy is outlined in this chapter. This combines goal-free, inductive, and theory-testing modes of investigation and offers options for practitioners operating under a range of budgetary and time constraints.

A second point noted in this chapter is that the weight and quality of evidence required to infer causality varies dramatically depending on the context in which the evaluation is being conducted. The usual standards from the social sciences (which are roughly equivalent to beyond a reasonable doubt) will be too lenient in some situations and too stringent in others. What is crucial is that the required level of certainty is ascertained by the evaluator early on in the evaluation planning stage, that estimates are made of what evidence is required to meet that standard, and that decisions are made as to whether theory-based or other approaches are used.

Finally, as Cook (Chapter Three) notes, theory-based evaluation should not be seen simply as a replacement for experimental and quasi-experimental designs. For high-stakes evaluations with large budgets and extended time lines, the two may be used in conjunction to allow virtually bulletproof causal attributions, provided they are used skillfully. For the everyday evaluator under more serious time and budgetary constraints, ideas from both methodologies should be considered in order to build evidence for inferring causality (see the list of potential types of evidence for inferring causality earlier in this chapter). The depth and breadth of the required evidence base is a key consideration in evaluation planning and should be based on a thorough assessment by the evaluator of stakeholder information needs. This not only will help with budgeting the evaluation more accurately but also will facilitate any up-front discussions with the client about the trade-offs between budgets, time lines, and the certainty of conclusions.

## References

Bickman, L. "The Functions of Program Theory." In L. Bickman (ed.), *Using Program Theory in Evaluation.* New Directions for Program Evaluation, no. 33. San Francisco: Jossey-Bass, 1987.

Chen, H. T. *Theory-Driven Evaluations.* Thousand Oaks, Calif.: Sage, 1990.

Cohen, J., and Cohen, C. *Applied Multiple Regression/Correlation Analysis for the Behavioral Sciences.* (2nd ed.) Hillsdale, N.J.: Erlbaum, 1983.

Cook, T. D., and Campbell, D. T. *Quasi-Experimentation: Design and Analysis Issues for Field Settings.* Skokie, Ill.: Rand McNally, 1979.

Cooksy, L. J. "The Meta-Evaluand: The Evaluation of Project Technology Enhancing Achievement in Middle School." *American Journal of Evaluation,* 1999, *20,* 123–136.

Donaldson, S. I., Graham, J. W., and Hansen, W. B. "Testing the Generalizability of Intervening Mechanism Theories: Understanding the Effects of Adolescent Drug Use Prevention Interventions." *Journal of Behavioral Medicine,* 1994, *17,* 195–216.

Ford, J. K., and others. "Process Tracing Methods: Contributions, Problems, and Neglected Research Questions." *Organizational Behavior and Human Decision Processes,* 1989, *43,* 75–117.

Huberman, A. M., and Miles, M. B. "Data Management and Analysis Methods." In N. K. Denzin and Y. S. Lincoln (eds.), *Collecting and Interpreting Qualitative Materials.* Thousand Oaks, Calif.: Sage, 1998.

Lipsey, M. "Theory as Method: Small Theories of Treatments." In L. Sechrest and A. Scott (eds.), *Understanding Causes and Generalizing About Them.* New Directions for Program Evaluation, no. 57. San Francisco: Jossey-Bass, 1993.

Miles, M. B., and Huberman, A. M. *Qualitative Data Analysis: An Expanded Sourcebook.* (2nd ed.) Thousand Oaks: Calif.: Sage, 1994.

Reynolds, A. J. "Confirmatory Program Evaluation: A Method for Strengthening Causal Inference." *American Journal of Evaluation,* 1998, *19,* 203–221.

Rogers, P. J., and McDonald, B. "Three Achilles Heels of Program Theory Evaluation." Paper presented at the international conference of the Australasian Evaluation Society, Perth, Australia, Oct. 1999.

Saxe, L., and Tighe, E. "The View from Main Street and the View from 40,000 Feet: Can a National Evaluation Understand Local Communities?" In J. Telfair, L. C. Leviton, and J. S. Merchant (eds.), *Evaluating Health and Human Service Programs in Community Settings.* New Directions for Evaluation, no. 83. San Francisco: Jossey-Bass, 1999.

Sayer, A. *Method in Social Science: A Realist Approach.* London: Routledge, 1992.

Scriven, M. "Maximizing the Power of Causal Investigation: The Modus Operandi Method." In W. J. Popham (ed.), *Evaluation in Education: Current Applications.* Berkeley, Calif.: McCutchan, 1974a.

Scriven, M. "Prose and Cons About Goal-Free Evaluation." In W. J. Popham (ed.), *Evaluation in Education: Current Applications.* Berkeley, Calif.: McCutchan, 1974b.

Scriven, M. *Evaluation Thesaurus.* (4th ed.) Thousand Oaks, Calif.: Sage, 1991.

Sosa, E., and Tooley, M. (eds.). *Causation.* New York: Oxford University Press, 1993.

Suchman, E. A. *Evaluative Research: Principles and Practice in Public Service and Social Action Programs.* New York: Russell Sage Foundation, 1967.

Weiss, C. H. *Evaluation Research: Methods of Assessing Program Effectiveness.* Englewood Cliffs, N.J.: Prentice Hall, 1972.

Weiss, C. H. "Theory-Based Evaluation: Past, Present, and Future." In D. J. Rog and D. Fournier (eds.), *Progress and Future Directions in Evaluation: Perspectives on Theory, Practice, and Methods.* New Directions for Evaluation, no. 76. San Francisco: Jossey-Bass, 1997.

*E. JANE DAVIDSON teaches consulting psychology at Alliant University/California School of Professional Psychology in San Diego and is completing a doctorate in evaluation and organizational behavior at Claremont Graduate University.*

**3**

*This chapter offers a critical commentary on theory-based evaluation, stressing its utility as a method of program planning and as an adjunct to experiments but rejecting it as an alternative to experiments.*

# The False Choice Between Theory-Based Evaluation and Experimentation

*Thomas D. Cook*

It is currently fashionable in many foundation and some scholarly circles to espouse a theory of evaluation for complex, aggregated social settings such as communities and schools that depends on three steps:

Explicating the substantive theory of the program to be evaluated so as to detail all the flow-through relationships that should occur if the intended intervention is to have an impact on major target outcomes. In education such outcomes include achievement gains, and in welfare policy they include stable employment in the labor force.

Collecting data from a relevant sample of units (usually people) and in this way measuring each of the constructs specified in the substantive theory of the program.

Analyzing the collected data in order to assess the extent to which the postulated relationships have actually occurred in the predicted time sequence. If the data collection can cover only part of the postulated causal chain, then only part of the model will be tested. However, the aspiration is to test the complete program theory.

One major reason that this theory of evaluation is currently in vogue is as much because of what it is not as because of what it is. It is *not* a theory of evaluation that depends solely on qualitative methods. Such a theory would lack credibility in many academic and policy circles if the results from the qualitative studies were used to support inferences about what a program has achieved for its clients or society at large. By contrast, the theory-based model seems scientific, acknowledging the importance of substantive theory, quantitative assessment, and causal modeling.

The theory-based approach to evaluation is also *not* experimental or even quasi-experimental. Advocates of theory-based evaluation point to how often experimental evaluations have produced disappointing results about community and school effects, leaving it unclear whether the programs are rarely effective or whether the experimental methods are too insensitive to register what a program has actually achieved. It is undeniable that there are very real and widely acknowledged practical difficulties that arise when doing real-world experiments with units higher than individuals, including communities and schools. It is therefore not illogical to want to shoot the messenger bearing the pessimistic message, leaving the message to live another day.

However, there are other reasons for preferring to shoot the messenger. If the message were correct, this would entail restricting or abandoning the cherished belief in *multiplier effects,* community-based forces that create impacts greater than the sum of individual effects. Belief in them sustains (and justifies) much of the funding aimed at intact communities and schools. So believing the messenger could also endanger the interests of the many program developers, researchers, and program funders whose reputations and jobs depend on "proper" evaluation making clear the general effectiveness of community-based interventions. But I do not want to be too cynical. It is also important to note that developers, funders, and researchers often encounter what they genuinely believe are effective projects during their visits to selected communities and schools. They see change occurring in these organizations, and they want a theory of evaluation that will register this change.

It is therefore a relief to them to learn of a theory of evaluation that claims to test causal effects validly, that promises to explain why these effects come about, and that does not concern itself with the inconvenient paraphernalia that experiments require in order to create a valid causal counterfactual against which to evaluate whether a program has caused any of the changes that might have been noted in a program group—namely, random assignment, close matching, pretests, and control groups. Espousing a theory of theory-based evaluation entails justifying research that includes the group experiencing the treatment and no one else. And its results will also seem scientific. If the causal modeling analyses suggest that the obtained data do not differ much from what the program theory predicts, then the presumption is that the validity of the theory and the success of the program have been demonstrated. Even if the time available for research does not permit assessing all the postulated causal links, the incomplete result can still be useful if it is congruent with the first part of the program theory. Such an incomplete result will at least inform staff about the quality of initial program implementation, as implementation variables are usually the first constructs in the causal model of the program. It can also be used against critics to argue for maintaining the program now that a data-based rationale exists for believing the program could be effective in the future. Moreover if the promised results are not initially obtained, then it is evidently illogical to argue that a program is effective because it sets in motion the postulated mediating processes. These have demonstrably not occurred. All this is the promise of theory-based evaluation—both the positive justification based on what it accomplishes and the negative justification based on avoiding the anticipated pessimism associated with most past experimental evaluations of community interventions.

The question I ask here is, Can theory-based evaluations provide the valid conclusions about a program's causal effects that have been promised? I will reply in the negative, citing at least seven reasons for skepticism. They all have to do with the network of assumptions on which theory-based evaluation is premised—that a highly specific program theory is available, that the measurement is of high quality, that valid analyses of explanatory time-dependent processes have been conducted, and that everyone understands what is logically entailed if only part of a model has been tested in the time frame available. I will then go on to argue that theory-based evaluation techniques are extremely useful when used together with experiments, rather than in opposition to them. When added to experiments, they will focus needed attention on what the program theory is, what level of program implementation is obtained, which presumed causal mediating processes actually change, and how this variation in implementation quality is related to variation in distal outcomes.

## Reasons for Skepticism

First, it was my experience in coauthoring a paper on the theory of a program with its developer (Anson and others, 1991) that program theories are not always very explicit. More important, in this case the theory could have been made more explicit in several different ways, not just one. Is there a single theory of a program, or are there several possible versions of it? I am definitely inclined from experience to favor the latter. And I do this not because of the obvious point that every program is dynamic and hence changing over time. Rather I would argue that it can be construed in multiple different ways even at any one time. This multiplicity of possible program theories entails a large (but not necessarily insurmountable) problem for a theory of theory-based evaluation.

Second, most of the program theories with which I am acquainted are very linear in their postulated flow of influence. They rarely incorporate reciprocal feedback loops or external contingencies that might moderate the entire flow of influence. Yet we know from bitter experience that how individuals have been affected by a program affects their subsequent exposure to the program, sometimes because they come to need it less and sometimes because they come to need it more. And we also know that programs do not exist in political, social, or cultural vacuums. They are contextually embedded, and these contexts affect how the programs work and how individuals and groups react to them. To postulate closed systems, clearly differentiated category boxes, and exclusively unidirectional causal arrows is all a little too neat for our chaotic world. It is better to assume constant external perturbations, constructs with fuzzy rather than clear boundaries, and causation that is reciprocal rather than unidirectional. Unfortunately, testing theories based on these more realistic but also more complex assumptions entails many more technical difficulties than testing simple linear models based on clearly independent constructs within a closed explanatory system.

Third, few program theories specify how long it should take for a given process to affect some proximal indicator in the causal chain. But without such specifications, it is difficult to know when a disconfirmation occurs, whether the next step in the model has simply not occurred yet or instead will not occur at all. It is this ambiguity about time lines that allows program developers who have been disappointed by evaluation results to claim that positive results would have occurred had the evaluation lasted longer. Given program theories with specific time lines, this particular argument would never be heard. But because such theories are not typically available, the argument is often heard when developers do not like what the evaluator reports. (This is not the fault of program developers, of course. The problem lies with the quality of our social science knowledge in general).

Fourth, theory-based evaluation places a great premium on knowing not just when to measure but how to measure. When measures are only partially valid, failure to corroborate a model is ambiguous in its implications. Does the failure reflect a program theory that is false—the desired inference—or does it reflect measures that were inadequate for a strong test of the theory? Researchers can protect against this dilemma by explicating constructs better initially, by choosing more reliable single measures, and by using multiple measures of the same construct. Although such procedures are always desirable in social research, they are probably nowhere more necessary than when using a theory-based approach to evaluation. It is unfortunate then that better and more extensive measurement costs money. In addition, it can be burdensome to respondents, including staff and students within communities and schools. Still, this objection based on the quality of measurement is essentially practical rather than theoretically fundamental, given that we can usually improve our measurement if we are willing to pay the opportunity costs. The major of these is that for a fixed budget fewer constructs will tend to be measured if it is important to raise the quality of assessment of individual constructs.

Fifth, there is the epistemological problem that many different models can usually be fit to any single pattern of data (Glymour, Scheines, Sprites, and Kelly, 1987). The causal modeling methods usually espoused by advocates of theory-based program evaluation do not permit falsifying among competing models. They do not allow us to ascertain whether different models with the same (or additional) variables would fit the data at least as well or better than the model under test. This leads to an apparent paradox. Theory-based evaluations are predicated on using theory to predict outcomes and not to explain how they came about, all appearances and rhetoric to the contrary. To discover a complex, multivariate pattern of data that matches what was predicted provides one plausible model of how the variables are interrelated but not necessarily the correct one.

The sixth and biggest problem with a theory of evaluation that depends on a program's substantive theory alone is that there is no valid counterfactual, no way of knowing what would have happened at any stage in the model had there not been the program. As a result, it is logically impossible to say whether any processes that are observed are genuine products of the intervention or whether they would have occurred anyway, even without the reform. How can we rule out all the threats to internal validity outlined in Cook and Campbell (1979)? The biggest struggle in evaluation is around summative claims—that is, claims that a program has or has not caused some observed consequence. Theory-based evaluation does not take on this central issue; it sidesteps it.

There is one circumstance, though, in which the claim has been made that causal inference can be justified without controlled assignment, control groups, pretests, and the like. This circumstance involves *signed causes* (Scriven, 1976), situations in which the postulated pattern of multivariate relationships is so unique that it could not have occurred other than through the availability of the reform. Unfortunately, signed causes depend on access to considerable well-validated substantive theory (Cook and Campbell, 1979). Detectives can "finger" a suspect because the crime scene provides a multivariate pattern of clues, because they already know the modus operandi (MO) of various suspects, because they presume to know all the relevant suspects using this MO, and because they can use interviews to discriminate among suspects if more than one of them has an MO matching the evidence at the crime scene. Likewise, pathologists can ascertain the cause of death because they have the multivariate evidence laid out before them on the dissecting table as a pattern of effects and because past research in anatomy, physiology, and the like has taught them how to identify the specific pathways through which individual diseases affect some organs but not others. Rarely do social scientists have such specific background information available to them from substantive theory and experience, so discriminating among alternative causes is much more difficult. And rarely is the pattern of effects to be explained as clear-cut as the crime scene that a detective finds or the body that a pathologist dissects. So the theory of signed causes is not likely to be a widely applicable alternative to a valid counterfactual control group. Indeed it is just an earlier form of theory-based evaluation.

So the best safeguard for those who place a high premium on identifying causal effects is to have at least one well-matched comparison group, and the best comparison group is a randomly constructed one. So we are back again with the proposition that theory-based evaluations are useful as complements to experiments but not as alternatives to them, and preferably as complements to randomized experiments rather than quasi-experiments.

My final reason for being against theory-based evaluation is not intrinsic to the method. But I do fear that it could be used to postpone doing hard-headed experimental work on programs. Many practical-minded advocates of specific reforms realize how difficult it will be to bring about substantial changes in distal outcomes, given inevitable shortfalls in program theory and implementation as well as in evaluation sensitivity, not to speak of the limitations associated with the short time lines within which change is often called for. The advocates' hope is that implementing a reform with vigor and theoretical fidelity will entail little dilution of influence across all the probabilistic links in a program's substantive theory. But their more realistic expectation—promises to funders notwithstanding—is that implementation will be weaker than desired and that some of the planned intervening processes may not come about even if the program theory is true. So it is tempting for program developers and those with a similar stake in the program's success to concentrate on the first steps in the program's theory, steps that refer to implementation issues and therefore seem to need control groups less urgently. However, if the initial steps in the theory do come about as planned, this will surely lead to the temptation to claim (illogically, as it happens) that later effects are more likely to come about because the earlier ones already have. Given the stakes and the probability of demonstrating success with distal-outcome criteria, it is easy to see how the advocacy of theory-based evaluation could become an excuse not to evaluate reforms by traditional summative means.

## Theory-Based Measurement and Analysis Within Experiments

I am resolutely in favor of evaluators measuring and analyzing theoretically specified mediating processes. If all the theories of a program that one can construct postulate relationships one knows to be generally false, then this indicates that the program is not likely to be worth much and is certainly not worth squandering evaluation resources on. Attention to program theory also helps place special emphasis on implementation quality. This is because the first variables in the causal sequence are the most often assessed, and they are usually tapped into implementation. It is my belief that evaluators with summative aspirations do not spend enough time dealing with implementation issues, even though implementation shortfalls are one important reason why results are often disappointing. Finally, I think that we need to know why programs are or are not effective. To learn this absolutely requires the measurement and analysis of data that are subsequent to implementation but prior to distal outcomes. So I am a fan of theory-based evaluation and have recently deliberately used the expression in the title of two articles (Cook and others, 2000; Cook, Hunt, and Murphy, 2000) evaluating Comer's School Development Program (Comer, 1980).

But these articles are about randomized experiments with whole schools as the unit of assignment and analysis. The studies were designed both to describe and to explain the program's consequences for school staff and students, using the randomized experiment part to describe causal relationships and using the theory-based part to help explain the pattern of results obtained. Thus I have tried to model ways of conducting evaluations that combine experimental designs and the analysis of such intervening processes as program implementation quality and early substantive process effects.

It is not easy to do experiments with intact communities and whole schools. There are many reasons for this, having to do with the sample size of units that one can afford to study and that are willing to participate, the highly variable program exposure within a setting, the treatment crossovers, the differential attrition, the politics and ethics of gaining access, the limitations of generalizations that arise from dealing only with settings willing to volunteer to be in the study, and so forth. I have yet to meet a perfect community or even school-based experimental evaluation, and my own studies certainly do not merit such an appellation. Particularly worrisome, in my view, is that experimental work with intact communities will often be very expensive if a sufficiently large number of communities is to be included in the design. One might even argue that the depressing picture of community-level effects that has emerged from experimental evaluations is deceptive, based on studies so small as to have little chance of showing effects. So experimental evaluation needs to be undertaken more often, taking advantage of all that has been learned about implementing randomized experiments over the last twenty years.

The great advantage of experiments (or of close approximations) is that the test, from the intervention to the individual intervening processes, is unbiased or involves less bias than the alternative approaches to evaluation. This is because experiments are designed to examine whether each step in the causal model is related to the planned treatment contrast. But a causal model involves other tests, especially of the path from intervening processes to the planned distal outcomes. These tests are potentially biased. In essence, they depend on stratifying units by the extent to which the postulated theoretical processes are faithfully reproduced before examining how this variation in implementation is related to variation in the outcome. Still, these second-stage observational analyses are well worth doing, though their results should be clearly labeled as more tentative than the results of any planned experimental contrast.

In this context, it is interesting to note that Angrist, Imbrens, and Rubin (1996) have argued that it is possible to obtain unbiased estimates of the consequences of intervening processes—but only when there is random assignment. This is because such assignment can function as an unbiased instrumental variable. So if they are correct, unbiased causal inferences are sometimes possible both from the treatment to the intervening variables and from the intervening variables to the distal outcomes. Unfortunately, the method of Angrist, Imbrens, and Rubin has not yet been generalized to handle the multiple different intervening variables that a program theory postulates will change at different times in a causal sequence. Hence we still need to conduct traditional causal modeling analyses of the pattern of influence from the intervention to the various mediating variables and then from these mediators to a distal outcome.

Few evaluators will argue against the more frequent and sophisticated use of substantive theory to detail intervening processes. Probably the sole exceptions are those who believe that the act of measuring process creates conditions different from those that would apply in the actual policy world. Few evaluators argue that it is not possible to collect measures of intervening processes. So it should be possible to construct and justify a theory-based form of evaluation that complements experiments and is in no way an alternative to them. It would prompt experimenters to be more thoughtful about how they conceptualize, measure, and analyze intervening process. It would also remind them of the need to first probe whether an intervention leads to changes in each of the theoretically specified intervening processes and then explore whether these processes could plausibly have caused changes in the more distal outcomes of policy interest. I want to see theory-based methods used *within* an experimental framework and not as an alternative to it.

### References

Angrist, J. D., Imbrens, G. W., and Rubin, D. B. "Identification of Causal Effects Using Instrumental Variables." *Journal of the American Statistical Association*, 1996, *91*, 444–462.

Anson, A., and others. "The Comer School Development Program: A Theoretical Analysis." *Journal of Urban Education*, 1991, *26*, 56–82.

Comer, J. P. *School Power*. New York: Free Press, 1980.

Cook, T. D., and Campbell, D. T. *Quasi-Experimentation: Design and Analysis Issues for Field Settings*. Boston: Houghton Mifflin, 1979.

Cook, T. D., Hunt, H. D., and Murphy, R. M. "Comer's School Development Program in Chicago: A Theory-Based Evaluation." *American Education Research Journal*, forthcoming, summer 2000.

Cook, T. D., and others. "Comer's School Development Program in Prince George's County, Maryland: A Theory-Based Evaluation." *American Educational Research Journal*, forthcoming, winter 2000.

Glymour, C., Scheines, R., Sprites, P., and Kelly, K. *Discovering Causal Structure: Artificial Intelligence, Philosophy of Science, and Statistical Modeling*. Orlando, Fla.: Academic Press, 1987.

Scriven, M. "Maximizing the Power of Causal Investigation: The Modus Operandi Method." In G. V. Glass (ed.), *Evaluation Studies Review Annual*. Thousand Oaks, Calif.: Sage, 1976.

*THOMAS D. COOK is professor of sociology at Northwestern University.*

4

*If there is little consensus about the assumptions under-
lying a program, theory-based evaluators can collect data
relevant to more than one theory, selecting for study the
specific links in those theories that answer key questions.*

# Which Links in Which Theories
# Shall We Evaluate?

*Carol Hirschon Weiss*

Theory-based evaluation (TBE) offers many advantages to the evaluator
who conducts the study and the program individuals who receive the
results. It helps to specify not only the *what* of program outcomes but also
the *how* and the *why*. Theory-based evaluation tests the links between
what programs assume their activities are accomplishing and what actually happens at each small step along the way. It also has clear limitations
(Weiss, 1997).

Other chapters in this issue explore the opportunities and challenges
that enter into the decision to use this approach to evaluating programs. I
want to enter the scene after all the actors have decided to take a theory-
oriented approach and now have to put the approach into practice. What
theory do they use? Do they settle on one theory, or do they consider several
theories? In how much detail do they spin out the theories? If they have an
elaborated theory (or theories), which links in the theory do they study?
What criteria do they use in deciding which links are worth studying?

## Studying the Mechanisms of Social Change

TBE is an effort to examine the mechanisms by which programs influence
successive stages of participants' behavior. Table 4.1 shows a possible theory of a job-training program. A theory-based evaluation can examine
whether trainees learn the skills taught, whether learning the skills leads
to the search for a job, whether the search for a job leads to interviews
with prospective employers, whether interviews lead to getting hired, and
so on.

NEW DIRECTIONS FOR EVALUATION, no. 87, Fall 2000 © Jossey-Bass

## Table 4.1. Theory of a Job-Training Program

Program publicizes a job-training program.
> Youth hear about the program.
> Youth are interested and motivated to apply.

Program enrolls eligible youth.
> Youth sign up.

Program provides occupational training in an accessible location.
> Youth attend regularly.

Training matches labor market needs.
Training is carried out well.
> Youth learn skills.

Training teaches good work habits.
> Youth internalize values of regular employment and appropriate behavior on the job.

Program refers youth to suitable jobs.
> Youth apply for jobs.
> Youth behave well in job interviews.
> Employers offer jobs.
> Youth accept jobs.
> Youth show up for work regularly.

Program assists youth in making transition to work and helps with problems.
> Youth accept authority on the job.
> Youth do their work well.
> Youth behave well with coworkers.
> Youth stay on the job.

*Source:* Adapted from Weiss, 1998, p. 59.

TBE is an attempt to see how far the program succeeds in accomplishing all the intervening phases between enrollment in the program and long-term job holding. If trainees do well all along the route from participation in the training program to staying on a job, there is at least plausible reason to believe that the program was responsible for the trainees' work success. (See Chapter Two by Jane Davidson for further discussion of establishing causality.)

But let us take a step back. Table 4.1 shows the expected steps in the implementation of the program. It is what might be called the *implementation theory* of the program. But why are the trainees going to follow through and wind up in long-term jobs? The table does not delve into underlying psychosocial mechanisms. What is going to keep the trainees engaged in what must seem at first an uncongenial period of training? Perhaps the youth are rational enough to want to acquire skills that will help them get ahead in the job market, or perhaps being with a group of peers provides the social support that keeps them engaged, or perhaps program staff instill a sense of group esprit and a sense of excitement about the benefits of work that support the youth in staying with the program.

These kinds of mechanisms are the things that will largely determine whether the implementation theory succeeds in moving through the steps described in Table 4.1 from the top to the bottom. They are what I would call the real *program theory*. Together, the implementation theory and the program theory can be called the *theory of change* that the program posits as its route to success.

## Which Theory to Select

Some programs are designed on an explicit theoretical basis, and a TBE can investigate whether the assumptions of the theory hold in practice. But many programs are the product of experience, intuition, and professional rules of thumb. A theory-based evaluator has to dig to uncover the implicit assumptions underlying the program. Often there are multiple views on what will make the program successful. Take a program that offers counseling to teenagers at risk of dropping out of school, for example. The counselors are young black and Latino men and women who grew up in the same inner-city neighborhood as the teenagers and studied counseling in a nearby community college. They are expected to steer the teens to a better awareness of the advantages of education and to encourage them to stay in school. Some people involved with the program also expect them to help the youth deal with difficult life circumstances, such as an abusive parent or involvement in gang activities. Some program people also expect them to intercede for troubled youth with social workers, police, or probation officers or to help the teens secure services from health clinics or other service agencies.

Several theories of action might be operating. Some people, maybe the program administrators, think that the counselors are role models for the teens. Because of common ethnic backgrounds and life circumstances, the teens can identify with them, will take their words of advice seriously, and will follow a more positive social path. Another theory might be that the counselors understand the perils and pressures that the teens face and will give advice that is better suited to the real world of the inner city than would a middle-class teacher or counselor. They will know how to advise on family problems because of the commonality of their family backgrounds. Another theory might be that the counselors, understanding the local culture, can use threats and penalties effectively, something that white middle-class counselors would be loath to do. Yet another theory is that the counselors will be well acquainted with all the available services in the community and therefore can refer the youth to an appropriate source of help. All of these assumptions grow from the match of counselors to the ethnic and socioeconomic status of the teenagers.

A different set of assumptions would refer to the specific steps and actions that the counselors use in their relations with the teens, perhaps growing from the particular training that they received in the community college. They may have received training in the use of rewards for small steps that a youth takes in a positive direction, such as offering a movie pass for attending school five days in a row. Or they may have been trained to help with the development of peer support groups, where a group of youngsters help one another maintain good school attendance and proper completion of schoolwork. One might also imagine that a counselor could be effective by tutoring young people in the subjects that give them the most trouble in school and help them overcome cognitive deficits. There are a plethora of theoretical bases on which one might expect the program to be successful in encouraging young people to remain in school and do good work.

If the evaluator is embarking on a theory-based evaluation, which theory does she[1] hook the study to? Does she follow the counselor's encouragement of school attendance? His intervention into family disputes? His referrals to service agencies? His establishment of support groups? His coaching in math? Or what? One study can rarely collect data on all possible activities and their cascading consequences. It would be burdensome to follow each chain of possible events, and the evaluation would become complex and ponderous. Choices have to be made. The evaluator has to decide which of the several theories to track through the series of subsequent steps.

Overall, there are two major sources of theory—the social science literature and the beliefs of program stakeholders. The advantage of social science theories is that they are likely to be based on a body of evidence that has been systematically collected and analyzed. The main disadvantage is that available social science theory may not match the program under review, and even when it does, it may be at such a high degree of abstraction that it is difficult to operationalize in the immediate context. Nevertheless, when social science provides theory and concepts that ground and support local formulations, it can be of great evaluative value (Chen and Rossi, 1987). The evaluator should bring her knowledge of the social science literature to bear on the evaluation at hand.

A way to begin the task of choosing a theory to follow is to ask the program designers, administrators, and practitioners how they believe the program will work. They may have clear-cut ideas about the chain of actions and reactions that they believe will lead to better school achievement of the youth. But it is not unusual to find that different people in the program hold different assumptions about the steps by which inputs will translate into desired outcomes. What can the evaluator do?

First, she can convene a meeting of the stakeholders in the program, perhaps including the youth who are the program's clients, and ask them to discuss their assumptions about how the program will reach the desired results. They should discuss the ministeps of counselor action and youth response that will lead to success. Through such discussion, their originally hazy ideas may become clear, and they may reach consensus about what the program truly aims to do and how it aims to do it.

Program staff will often find a discussion of this type revealing and eminently practical. They will learn what their colleagues assume should be done (and what they are doing). Staff may all be performing the same functions but doing them with different assumptions about why they will be successful. Or they may actually be doing different things. In discussion, they can find out whether they are working at cross-purposes or are on the same wavelength. If they are working in different directions, the program is apt to be fragmented and ineffective. Staff will often find the effort to reach consensus a stimulating and useful exercise. It may help the program attain coherence and direction.

## Including Several Theories

In some instances, some program staffs cannot reach consensus. They have markedly different theories about where they should put their time and what kind of actions they should take in order to engage problem youth in school. In such cases, it may be necessary to include several different theories in the evaluation design. The evaluation can follow the chains of assumption of several theories to see which of them is best supported by the data.

When a number of different assumptions are jostling for priority, a TBE is wise to include multiple theories. If only one theory is tracked, and that theory is wrong or incomplete, the evaluator may miss important chains of action. The final result may show that positive outcomes were achieved but not through the series of steps posited by the theory. The evaluator will be unable to explain how success was attained (see Brug, Steenhuis, Van Assema, and De Vries 1996; Puska, Nissinen, and Tuomilehto, 1985). Or if the program has disappointing results, and only one theory was tracked, the evaluator may face readers who say, "But that's not how we thought good results would come about anyway." When programs rest on fuzzy assumptions, it is often useful for TBE to represent a range of theoretical expectations.

But the more theories that are tracked, the more complex and expensive the evaluation. It is worthwhile to try to winnow down the number of possible theories to a manageable number. Three or four would seem to be the maximum that an evaluator could explore in a single study. How can the evaluator decide which of the several theories is worth including in the evaluation?

## Criteria for Selecting Theories

The first criterion is the beliefs of the people associated with the program, primarily the designers and developers who planned the program, the administrators who manage it, and the practitioners who carry it out on a daily basis. Also important may be the beliefs of the sponsors whose money funds the program and the clients who receive the services of the program. What do these groups assume are the pathways to good outcomes? What are the ministeps that have to be taken if the clients are to reap the benefits that the program promises? What the people who are deeply involved in the program believe is critical because their behavior largely determines how the program runs. When they hold divergent assumptions about the route to success, the several theories that they proffer become candidates for inclusion.

A second criterion is plausibility. Can the program actually do the things that a theory assumes, and will the clients be likely to respond in the expected fashion? The evaluator needs to see what is really going on. One way is to follow the money. Where is the budget being spent? Where is the program really putting its chips? Which resources are they providing for what kinds of assistance? If the program makes available to each counselor a list of accessible service agencies, their eligibility criteria, and hours of operation, then it is a reasonable bet that they think the referral route is important. If nobody gives the counselors any information about available resources, then this theory is probably not an active candidate for study. If program designers and administrators talk a good deal about ethnic match between counselor and client but end up hiring primarily white middle-class counselors, ethnic match is not an operative theory in this program. Similarly, if the counselors do not know enough about plane geometry or nineteenth-century American history to tutor youth, then assumptions about success through tutoring are not apt to be the route to follow (unless the counselors find other people to do the tutoring). The evaluator needs to take a hard look at the program in action, not just in its planning documents, in order to see which theories are at least plausible in this location.

A third criterion is lack of knowledge in the program field. For example, many programs seem to assume that providing information to program participants will lead to a change in their knowledge, and increased knowledge will lead to a positive change in behavior. This theory is the basis for a wide range of programs, including those that aim to reduce the use of drugs, prevent unwanted pregnancy, improve patients' adherence to medical regimens, and so forth. Program people assume that if you tell participants about the evil effects of illegal drugs, the difficult long-term consequences of unwed pregnancies, and the benefits of complying with physician orders, they will become more conscious of consequences, think more carefully before embarking on dangerous courses of action, and eventually behave in more socially acceptable ways.

The theory seems commonsensical. But social scientists—and many program people—know that it is too simplistic. Much research and evaluation has cast doubt on its universal applicability. Although some programs that convey knowledge in an effort to change behavior have had good results, many have been notoriously unsuccessful. In an effort to add to the stock of knowledge in the program arena, an evaluator may find it worthwhile to pursue this theory in the context of the particular program with which she is working. She may want to carefully track the conditions of the program in order to gather more information about when and where such a theory is supported or disconfirmed by the evidence (and what elements of context, internal organization, and reinforcement make a difference).

So much effort is expended in providing information in an attempt to change behavior (through public service campaigns, material posted to Web sites, distribution of printed materials, lectures and speeches, courses and discussion groups, promotional messages disseminated through multiple media) that careful investigation of this theory is warranted. Furthermore so much uncertainty exists about the efficacy of providing information of different kinds to different audiences that program developers need a better sense of the prospects. The evaluator who pursues this theory in a TBE may look to social science theory for a sophisticated understanding of when and where information is likely to have effects and under what circumstances. She can build this knowledge into the evaluation. When the results of the evaluation are ready, she can offer program developers and staff a greater understanding of the extent to which information creates change within the immediate program context. Many studies have shown that information can lead to change in knowledge and attitudes but not often to change in behavior. The current evaluation can examine whether and where the sequence of steps in the theory breaks down and what forces undermine—or reinforce—the power of information.

A final criterion for choosing which theories to examine in a theory-based evaluation is the centrality of the theory to the program. Some theories are so essential to the operation of a program that no matter what else happens, the program's success hinges on the viability of this particular theory. Let us take the example of a comprehensive community program. The program involves the provision of funds (by government or a foundation) to a group of community residents, who then decide which enhancements the neighborhood needs in order to improve the lot of its inhabitants. The residents can choose to use the funds to add more services (mental health, education, and so on), clean up the streets and parks, rehabilitate buildings, hire private police, attract new business to the neighborhood in order to create jobs for local people, begin a car service for elderly residents, or whatever other services they decide are most likely to improve the local quality of life.

An evaluation can study the services chosen and find out the consequences of adding police or rehabilitating buildings or whatever other new services have been added. But a fundamental premise of this community-based approach is that local residents are knowledgeable, committed, hard working, and altruistic enough to find out what is most needed and to go about getting those services into the community. Further, they are assumed to represent the needs and wants of a wide swath of the community. So an underlying theory has to do with the role of citizen groups in developing and directing a comprehensive community initiative. The effectiveness of a group of residents in representing the interests of their neighborhood and securing priority services is key to the success of the program. This assumption becomes a prime candidate for the evaluation.

## Which Links in a Theory to Study

Many theories, if drawn out in detail, consist of a long series of interlinked assumptions about how a program will achieve its effects. Let us go back to the job-training program in Table 4.1. If the evaluation does not have the resources or the time to study all of the steps laid out in the theory, which of them should the evaluation explore? Much of the answer to this question will depend on the practicalities of the situation. At what point is the evaluator brought to the scene? Is it after the first several steps have already been taken? How much money does the evaluation have to collect data? How difficult is it to get some kinds of data? For example, what kind of data will the evaluator need in order to know whether the training is carried out well? How will she find out whether the trainees adopt and internalize the values of regular employment? If some kinds of data are difficult or expensive to collect, that will set practical limits.

Second, program staff may have particular concerns about some segments of the implementation theory. They may want to know, for example, whether trainers are giving proper emphasis to good work habits and other "soft skills" or whether the youth in fact learn the occupational skills that the trainers seek to convey. They may want to know whether staff refer them to relevant jobs and whether the youth comport themselves appropriately in job interviews, so that it is clear why they do or do not get jobs.

It may be even more important to examine some links in the program theory about the psychosocial processes that underlie the program. Here is where much of the uncertainty in social programming lies. What impels developing countries to seek to attract more girls into the school system? What gets faculty members in urban universities to teach in interdisciplinary courses in order to retain students in school? In our example, what are the reasons that trainees persist in the training course and learn both job skills and work readiness skills? Is it the capacity of the trainers to develop supportive communities among the youth? Is it the strength of external rewards and punishments?

An evaluation can concentrate on understanding these kinds of mechanisms and the extent to which they operate within the program milieu. The evaluator can collect data on whether peer groups develop during the course of training and the messages and supports that these groups provide to their members. Do youth affiliate in subgroups? Do members of the various groups support the aims of the training program? (Or do they denigrate the effort to learn skills that will yield "chump change"?) Do the trainers actively encourage the formation of subgroups and provide leadership? What messages circulate in the different subgroups about the value of work and the willingness to accept authority on the job? Regarding the theory about external threats, how important to participants in the training program is the reduction in safety net supports?

Because evaluations to date have told their readers relatively little about the *why* of program success and failure, such inquiries may have great resonance. Studies that explore the psychosocial processes of program theory will have much to tell program designers, lessons (however tentative) that may be suggestive for a whole range of programs.

## Criteria for Selecting the Links to Study

The criteria for choosing which links to study are similar to the criteria for choosing which theories to study. Two are probably most important. The first criterion is the link or links that are most critical to the success of the program. It seems wise to invest resources in studying the particular assumption on which the program most basically rests. If the program is predicated on the assumption that what keeps youth enrolled in the full training program is the support of their peers, then that assumption warrants investigation.

The second criterion is the degree of uncertainty about the linkage. If nobody knows whether the assumption is likely to be supported empirically, or if prior studies have produced conflicting findings on the subject, that link may be worthy of systematic study. Some linkages are unsettled in the social science and the evaluation literatures. Some linkages seem to be supported in the social science literature (or in common sense), but evaluations of earlier programs show that they do not work in practice. An example would be the premise of case management within a multiservice program. A large number of multiservice programs have employed case managers who analyze the services that a family needs, locate and coordinate a range of services, and help the family members obtain appropriate services from relevant agencies. The idea of a family coordinator, an advocate and consultant to the family, sounds so utterly sensible that it is unsettling to find that evaluations have usually not found such programs successful (for example, Bickman and others, 1995; St. Pierre, Layzer, and Goodson, 1997). What are the assumptions that underlie case management? What is the case manager assumed to do, with what immediate consequences, leading to what next steps, with what later consequences? Including some of these kinds of links in the evaluation would yield important information.

## Conclusion

In selecting the theory or theories to use as scaffolding for a TBE, the evaluator should consider these criteria.

- The assumptions of the people associated with the program. What are their constructions of the interlinked steps by which program inputs are transmuted into program outcomes?
- The plausibility of the assumptions, given the manner in which the program is allocating its time and resources.
- Uncertainty about the applicability of current assumptions. Given the often inchoate or contested nature of available evidence, do these assumptions hold? Under what conditions do they hold?

- The centrality of the assumptions to the program. If the program is based directly on a particular theory, it would be sensible to make this theory the centerpiece of the TBE.

Once the evaluator decides which theory or theories to use for structuring the evaluation, she ought to spell out all the links in the theory chain—what the program will do, how participants will respond, what the program does next, and so on. Many evaluations will not realistically be able to follow all the links in each chain, and the evaluator needs to choose the links on which to focus. Considerations for making that choice include the practicalities of access, resources, and methodological capability for studying given links and the particular knowledge needs of program staff, who want to know which elements of the program they need to modify or shore up.

In making both choices—which theories to select and which links to study—the evaluator needs to consider the underlying *mechanisms* on which the program rests, what I have called the *program theory* in contradistinction to the *implementation theory*. In some cases, the strongest contribution that TBE can make will be to analyze the psychosocial and political assumptions that undergird the program. TBE can then answer the question *why* as well as *how*.

I doubt that TBE should be a routine part of every evaluation. In many programs and for many purposes, an investigation of theoretical assumptions is too elaborate, too demanding, and probably irrelevant. What many program sponsors and managers want to know can be discovered by simpler and less probing strategies. But I also believe that TBE need not be the exhaustive and exhausting exercise that its image sometimes evokes. It can be domesticated and housebroken to fit even quite routine needs, as long as a key interest is *how* and *why* observed results come out the way they do.

It would be nice to think that over time repeated evaluations of a particular kind of program will yield consistent evidence about the validity of the theories on which the program is based, whether pro or con. In my most optimistic moments, I succumb to the notion that evaluations may be able to pin down which links in which theories are generally supported by evidence and that program designers can make use of such understanding in modifying current programs and planning new ones. I would like to believe that replicated evaluations can explain why some apparently commonsensical program strategies fail to work time after time and thus give clues for program improvement. Such hopes are no doubt too sunny. Given the astronomical variety of implementations of even one basic program model, the variety of staffs, clients, organizational contexts, social and political environments, and funding levels, any hope for deriving generalizable findings is romantic. Nevertheless, theory-based evaluation can add to knowledge. Even relatively small increments of knowledge about how and why programs work or fail to work cannot help but improve program effectiveness. And that is what program evaluation is all about.

## Note

1. In this chapter, I use the feminine pronoun to refer to the evaluator and the masculine pronoun for all other actors to avoid the awkward "he or she" construction.

## References

Bickman, L., Noser, K., and Summerfelt, W. T. "Long-Term Effects of a System of Care on Children and Adolescents." *Journal of Behavioral Health Services and Research*, 1999, 26(2), 185–202.

Bickman, L., and others. *Evaluating Managed Mental Health Services: The Fort Bragg Experiment.* New York: Plenum, 1995.

Brug, J., Steenhuis, I., Van Assema, P., and De Vries, H. "The Impact of a Computer-Tailored Nutrition Intervention." *Preventive Medicine*, 1996, 25, 236–242.

Chen, H. T., and Rossi, P. H. "The Theory-Driven Approach to Validity." *Evaluation and Program Planning*, 1987, 10, 95–103.

Puska, P., Nissinen, A., and Tuomilehto, J. "The Community-Based Strategy to Prevent Coronary Heart Disease: Conclusions for the Ten Years of the North Karelia Projects." *Annual Review of Public Health*, 1985, 6, 147–193.

St. Pierre, R. G., Layzer, J. I., Goodson, B. D., and Bernstein, L. S. *National Impact Evaluation of the Comprehensive Child Development Program: Final Report.* Cambridge, Mass.: Abt Associates, 1997.

Weiss, C. H. "How Can Theory-Based Evaluation Make Greater Headway?" *Evaluation Review*, 1997, 21, 501–524.

Weiss, C. H. *Evaluation: Methods for Studying Programs and Policies.* (2d ed.) Englewood Cliffs, N.J.: Prentice Hall, 1998.

*CAROL HIRSCHON WEISS is professor of education at the Harvard Graduate School of Education.*

5

*Program evaluations can be based on different causal
models to suit different purposes. This chapter discusses
several types of causal relationships, three causal models
derived from systems theory, and the role that causal
models play in program theory evaluation.*

# Causal Models in Program
# Theory Evaluation

*Patricia J. Rogers*

Causal models are at the heart of program theory evaluation, yet there has
been surprisingly little discussion of the different types of causal relationships that might be operating in a causal model nor of the different types of
causal models that might be useful for program evaluation (exceptions being
Lipsey and Pollard, 1989; McClintock, 1990). This chapter begins by discussing the different types of causal relationships that we might want to represent in our causal models and how we might develop standardized ways
to represent these visually. It then briefly explores how nonlinear causal
models from systems theory might be used for program theory evaluation.
The chapter finishes by discussing the role that causal models play in program theory evaluation. As these various models each highlight different
issues that may be important in understanding how outcomes were achieved
(or not achieved), it may sometimes be appropriate to use a series of different causal models over several cycles of evaluation or monitoring.

Chen (1990) distinguished between two different types of causal
model—*normative* (how the program is understood to work) and *descriptive* (how the program actually works). The issues raised in this chapter can
be applied to either normative models or descriptive models.

*Note:* This chapter has benefited substantially from the helpful comments, questions,
and suggestions from members of the Harvard Evaluation Task Force, participants at
the 1998 American Evaluation Association meeting, the editors and series editor of this
volume, and as always my graduate evaluation students. Initial work on this chapter was
supported by a fellowship from the Spencer Foundation.

## What Do the Boxes and Arrows Represent?

Program theory usually involves a diagram of boxes linked by arrows representing cause-and-effect relationships. It is perhaps tempting to consider these causal models to be like wiring diagrams, in which, if we flick a switch at the first box in the diagram, it will cause the lights in the other boxes to illuminate. And indeed, sometimes the descriptions of these models, using a series of if-then statements, suggest this imagery (Owen, with Rogers, 1999; Plantz, Greenway, and Hendricks, 1997).

Evaluators who are familiar with social science principles will not be surprised that few program theory models are based on simple causal relationships like this, even if diagrams do not explicitly show it. However, some program theory models do explicitly attempt to show the processes that are "necessary and sufficient" to produce the desired results—for example, Cooley's causal model (1997) of a program designed to increase girls' participation in high school in developing countries.

More commonly, program theory models are based on a recognition that other factors may influence the achievement of intermediate and ultimate outcomes. For example, the United Way's generic causal model does not explicitly include other factors, apart from a list of constraints on the program. However, in the instructions provided with this model, it is made clear that the further away from actual program outputs one moves, the weaker the program's influence becomes, and the likelihood of outside forces having an influence increases (Plantz, Greenway, and Hendricks, 1997). They go on to give an example of a program providing prenatal counseling for pregnant teens, pointing out that the program can influence what pregnant teens know about appropriate prenatal practices but cannot influence what the teens' overall health was when they became pregnant. Nor can the programs affect whether teens were using drugs when they became pregnant. The authors recognize that each of these issues, general health and involvement with drugs, can have as much long-term influence on the later health of babies as the program itself.

It is interesting to note that this analysis focuses only on fixed characteristics or events that happen before the client begins in the program—sometimes referred to as *moderators*. Outcomes can also be influenced by factors that occur at the same time as the program and either help or hinder its work.

How can we represent these other factors in our causal models? Funnell's program theory matrix (Chapter Nine) includes other factors explicitly in text associated with each outcome. It is also possible to show them on the program theory diagram, as Halpern (1998, 1999) has done, as seen in Figure 5.1.

We might even make a dramatic move completely away from our program-centric causal model and show the web of client relationships that influence client outcomes, including the influence of family, friends, schools, shops, economy, neighborhood, media, legal system, work, economy, and political system (Bullen, 1995).

**Figure 5.1.  Representing Other Factors in a Logic Model for Reducing Alcohol-Related Motor Vehicle Accident Injuries and Deaths**

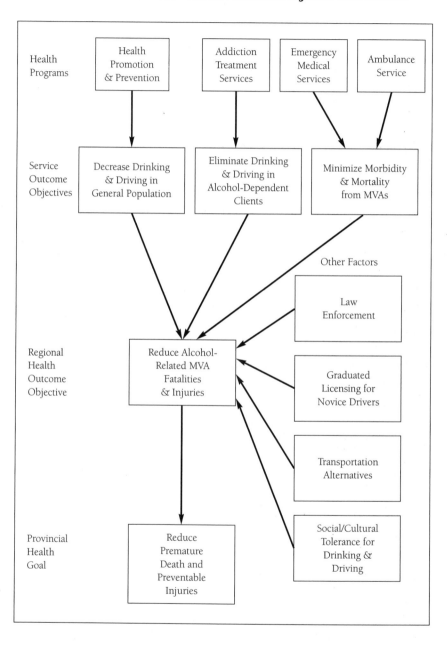

*Source:* Halpern, 1998, 1999.

## Multiple Strands in Causal Models

Many program theory models portray the program as a single chain of intermediate and ultimate outcomes, where A leads to B and then to C. But it
may be helpful to show multiple strands, where A and C both lead to B—
either in combination or as alternatives. Ideally, we would be able to distinguish between complementary causal paths and alternative causal paths in
a diagram, perhaps by using line arrows for the complementary paths and
block arrows for the alternative paths.

If a combination of two causal paths is necessary to achieve the intended
results, it is important to make this explicit in order to avoid maximizing only
one of them. In many programs, staff must balance competing imperatives like
this. When I worked with maternal and child health nurses to develop a causal
model of their program to guide the development of performance indicators,
they were particularly pleased that they could make visible the balancing they
needed to maintain between providing information to parents and supporting
parents' confidence in their own abilities. Part of their program model, which
used an adaptation of Bennett's hierarchy (Bennett and Rockwell, 1999) to
describe their work on infant feeding, showed this clearly, as seen in Figure 5.2.

It was important for the staff to make visible to program managers the
competing demands on them and to make sure that performance measures
referred to both of these in order to ensure that there were not structural

**Figure 5.2. A Partial Program Model Showing Competing Demands**

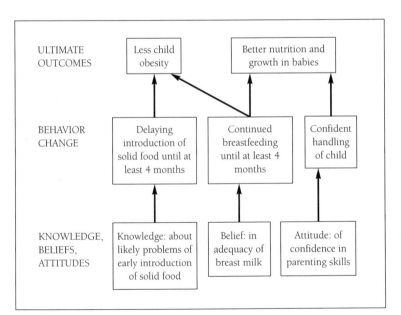

pressures to maximize either information giving or parental support at the expense of the other. When programs are managed by managers without detailed knowledge of program processes or are managed through contractual arrangements, it becomes more important to make explicit competing imperatives such as these. If performance measures only include one of the competing imperatives, then a program may seem to be performing well in terms of its intermediate outcomes because one of these is being maximized at the expense of the other.

Multiple strands in a causal model may instead represent alternative causal paths. For example, Weiss (1998) outlines four possible mechanisms by which higher teacher pay may be linked to increased student achievement. If these are seen as competing explanations for observed outcomes, then a program theory evaluation might focus on testing which of these best explains the evidence (as Weiss discusses in Chapter Four).

It is also possible to see these alternative causal paths as being true for certain people under certain conditions. Drawing an analogy with gunpowder, which will only fire in favorable conditions, Pawson and Tilley (1997) have suggested that program causal mechanisms only fire within favorable contexts. An evaluation based on this type of causal model will try to understand the circumstances under which particular mechanisms operate. In their reanalysis of a crime prevention program in public housing estates, Pawson and Tilley (1997) demonstrated the importance of understanding the context at different sites, including interactions among various mechanisms (such as improved housing and increased tenant involvement in estate management) and among other coexisting processes.

It is difficult to represent these more complex relationships in a two-dimensional diagram. Pawson and Tilley (1997) instead represent their causal model in a matrix of context-mechanism-outcome configurations, which describes in text the causal mechanism that produces the outcome and the context in which the mechanism is operative.

The characteristics of program clients—their motivations, attitudes, previous knowledge, and skills—are an important part of the context within which causal mechanisms work or fail to work. An iterative series of data collection and analysis activities can be used to identify important ways in which clients vary and the implications of these for program effectiveness (McDonald and Rogers, 1999).

To fully understand the context within which causal mechanisms operate, we may need to develop program models that do more than include program clients simply as passive recipients of treatments that change their lives. If the treatment involves swallowing a pill, we might expect certain physiological effects, regardless of the active involvement of the patient, but even in this example, we know that the patient's expectations about the treatment can influence its reported impacts. It is even less realistic to describe program clients as passive recipients when the program is endeavoring to bring about permanent change in, for example, students' school behavior or communication strategies of the hearing impaired—changes that require program clients to learn, apply, and maintain new ways of operating.

Pawson and Tilley (1997) have argued that we need "to shake off those conceptual habits which allow us to speak of a program 'producing outcomes' and to replace them with an imagery which sees the program offering chances which may (or may not) be triggered into action via the subject's capacity to make choices. . . . Potential subjects will consider a program (or not), volunteer for it (or not), cooperate closely (or not), stay the course (or not), learn lessons (or not), retain the lessons (or not), apply the lessons (or not)" (p. 38).

This issue does not need to be associated with a philosophical commitment to serving program clients and having their needs and perspectives at the forefront of program planning and evaluation nor with a belief that the personal dignity of clients and staff requires treating them as program partners rather than as passive objects. In fact, the same distinction holds true for programs such as burglary prevention, which intend to change the behavior of potential burglars. Programs can be understood as changing the options available to participants and their capacities to choose and enact these choices. Usually programs seek to increase options and capacities; some, such as burglary prevention, seek to reduce them.

## Causal Models from Systems Theory

Systems theory suggests other types of causal models. In this section, I discuss three of these that appear to be potentially useful for program evaluation—virtuous or vicious circles, symptomatic solutions, and feedback delays.

**Virtuous or Vicious Circles.**  Systems thinking suggests that cause and effect might often be connected not in a linear way but in a circular way, through a series of *virtuous circles* (where an initial effect leads to its own reinforcement and magnification) or *vicious circles* (where an initial negative effect is similarly magnified).

Funnell (1997) has discussed how process feedback loops may be important in a program model to show, for example, how attitudes may affect behavior, which may then affect attitudes further through processes of self-attribution. Other feedback loops may exist between the achievement of positive results from a program and its ability to attract clients. Batterham, Dunt, and Disler (1996), in their discussion of the evaluation of rehabilitation programs, discussed a similar process of iteration until a critical level of rehabilitation is reached (for example, independent mobility), at which point the client is able to move onto a further stage.

In terms of achieving ultimate outcomes, the presence of iterative causal mechanisms may not be important, providing that both the program and the evaluation continue for long enough for these effects to take place and be measured. Problems arise, however, when the program is not continued for long enough for the subsequent cycles of improvement to occur or when the evaluation is terminated before the ultimate outcomes are demonstrated. If a program sets in place an iterative virtuous circle, then it is possible that initially small gains may ultimately become significant. It is worth considering whether the outcomes of the program are likely to decay over time or to become stronger.

**Symptomatic Solutions.** *Symptomatic solutions* are solutions that relieve the symptoms but that actually make it harder to solve the problem. It would be like having the flu and taking tablets to reduce the symptoms and then continuing to work excessively, rather than convalescing, thereby making it harder to actually recover.

This problem has implications both for evaluation and for monitoring. For an evaluation, where we are trying to understand how effective a particular program has been in solving a problem, we should design our evaluation so that it can distinguish between temporary reduction of symptoms and sustainable solving of the problem. For monitoring, where we are seeking to simultaneously understand and influence program implementation, we should set up systems that do not encourage people to develop dysfunctional symptomatic solutions.

Owen and Lambert (1995) addressed this issue in their evaluation of a program in which all grade-five students used their individual notebook computers in all subjects. One of the unintended consequences of this program was an increase in teacher stress, as teachers struggled to develop their computer skills and simultaneously adapt their teaching material and processes. Initially, teachers responded to this increased stress by "getting on with the job," avoiding spending time in coordination meetings, or liaising with other teachers, and the administration sought to support teachers by leaving them alone and not making additional calls on their time. If the evaluation had measured teacher stress at this point only, it would have found that in the short-term teacher stress was reduced through this coping mechanism. But over time, this symptomatic solution led to hoarding of equipment, rivalry among groups, and poor attendance at information sessions—consequences that made it harder to implement the fundamental solution, which involved better sharing and coordination of resources and increased support and training for teachers.

**Feedback Delays.** We have probably all experienced the effects of *feedback delay* when trying to adjust the water temperature in a shower. If there is a delay in response, we tend to overcorrect—first too hot, then too cold, until eventually reaching the desired equilibrium. The Massachusetts Institute of Technology "beer game" simulation (Senge, 1990) has demonstrated the effects of feedback delay on a simple program—a system for producing and distributing a single brand of beer. Once there is a delay built into the system, so that the decision makers do not immediately see the impact of the changes they are making, the orders become more and more excessive and unbalanced.

The reason for using performance measures and indicators as part of ongoing evaluation in the public sector is that they can be used by managers to take corrective action in programs, much like someone monitoring and adjusting the shower temperature. Unfortunately, few if any of these systems address the problem of feedback delay. In fact, I have been unable to find a single example that does.

## How Complex Should Program Theory Models Be?

Although this chapter has focused on more complex models and causal relationships, it is worth remembering that simple models can often be helpful, particularly in programs in which there have previously been few explicit conceptual and empirical connections made between program activities and outcomes. Building a plausible model of how the program is meant to work helps managers identify the most important processes or intermediate outcomes and focus their measurement and attention there. Given that many program evaluations still collect little data about program implementation or intermediate outcomes, there is often considerable value (as Lipsey, 1993; and Petrosino, Chapter Six, point out) in using even a simple two-step program model that simply identifies and measures one mediating variable that is understood to be necessary for the achievement of the ultimate outcomes. And having a common model of how the program is meant to work can help program staff work together and focus on those activities that are most important for program success.

In fact, as Weick (1995) argues, a model might provide a useful heuristic for purposeful action without necessarily being correct. He recounts the story of the reconnaissance unit, lost in the snow in the Swiss Alps for three days in a blizzard, who eventually managed to find their way safely back to camp with the help of a map—a map, they later discovered, of the Pyrenees, not of the Alps. "This incident raises the intriguing possibility that when you are lost, any old map will do. . . . Once people begin to act, . . . they generate tangible outcomes . . . in some context . . . and this helps them discover . . . what is occurring, . . . what needs to be explained, . . . and what should be done next" (pp. 54–55). Weick goes on to quote Sutcliffe, "Having an accurate environmental map may be less important than having some map that brings order to the world and prompts action" (pp. 56–57).

This analysis may well explain the positive responses that program staff often have to program theory evaluation (see, for example, Huebner, Chapter Eight), even when this is based on very simple causal models. But simple causal models can be dysfunctional in high-stakes evaluations that are linked to organizational incentive structures such as performance-pay or to summative evaluations that inform decisions about ending or continuing programs.

## Conclusion

This chapter has outlined a wider repertoire of causal models for evaluators to use to guide their evaluations. In using these models, we should remember that *any* causal model is indeed only a model—a simplification of reality to help us understand, predict, make decisions, and act. Rather than searching for the true causal model that underpins a program, evaluators might understand a program more by using a variety of causal models.

## References

Batterham, R., Dunt, D., and Disler, P. "Can We Achieve Accountability for Long-Term Outcomes?" *Archives of Physical Medicine and Rehabilitation,* 1996, 77, 1219–1225.

Bennett, C. F., and Rockwell, K. "Targeting Outcomes of Programs (TOP): A Hierarchy for Targeting Outcomes and Evaluating Their Achievement." [http://deal.unl.edu/TOP/synopsis.html]. 1999.

Bullen, P. "Evaluating Human Services: Complexity—Uncertainty—Self-Delusion—Rigour." *Evaluation News and Comment,* 1995, 3(2), 3–10. [available at http://www.mapl.com.au/A1.htm].

Chen, H. T. *Theory-Driven Evaluation.* Thousand Oaks, Calif.: Sage, 1990.

Cooley, L. Presentation to the Washington Evaluators' Conference, 1997.

Funnell, S. "Program Logic: An Adaptable Tool." *Evaluation News and Comment,* 1997, 6(1), 5–17.

Halpern, G. "From Hubris to Reality: Evaluating Innovative Programs in Public Institutions." *Innovation Journal: The Public Sector Innovation Journal,* Nov. 1998, revised Nov. 1999. [available at http://www.innovationcc/rev_arts/halp4.htm].

Lipsey, M. "Theory as Method: Small Theories of Treatments." In L. Sechrest and A. Scott (eds.), *Understanding Causes and Generalizing About Them.* New Directions for Program Evaluation, no. 57. San Francisco: Jossey-Bass, 1993.

Lipsey M., and Pollard, J. "Driving Toward Theory in Program Evaluation: More Models to Choose From." *Evaluation and Program Planning,* 1989, 12, 317–328.

McClintock, C. "Administrators as Applied Theorists." In L. Bickman (ed.), *New Directions for Evaluation: Advances in Program Theory.* New Directions for Program Evaluation, no. 47. San Francisco: Jossey-Bass, 1990.

McDonald, B., and Rogers, P. "Market Segmentation as an Analogy for Differentiated Program Theory: An Example from the Dairy Industry." Paper presented at the annual meeting of the American Evaluation Association, Orlando, Fla., 1999.

Owen, J. M., with Rogers, P. J. *Program Evaluation: Forms and Approaches.* Thousand Oaks, Calif.: Sage, 1999.

Owen, J. M., and Lambert, F. C. "Roles for Evaluation in learning Organizations." *Evaluation,* 1995, 1(2), 237–250.

Pawson, R., and Tilley, N. *Realistic Evaluation.* Thousand Oaks, Calif.: Sage, 1997.

Plantz, M. C., Greenway, M. T., and Hendricks, M. "Outcome Measurement: Showing Results in the Nonprofit Sector." In K. E. Newcomer (ed.), *Using Performance Measurement to Improve Public and Nonprofit Programs.* New Directions for Evaluation, no 75. San Francisco: Jossey-Bass, 1997.

Senge, P. M. *The Fifth Discipline: The Art and Practice of the Learning Organization.* New York: Doubleday, 1990.

Weick, K. E. *Sensemaking in Organizations.* Thousand Oaks, Calif.: Sage, 1995.

Weiss, C. H. *Evaluation: Methods for Studying Programs and Policies.* (2nd ed.) Englewood Cliffs, N.J.: Prentice Hall.

*PATRICIA J. ROGERS is director of the Program for Public Sector Evaluation in the Faculty of Applied Science, Royal Melbourne Institute of Technology, Australia.*

# PART TWO

## Opportunities

6

*Even simple program theory evaluations could be used in meta-analysis to provide benefit. Several examples of ways to combine the two are explored, including a hypothetical model and an actual example of a federal funding program.*

# Whether and Why? The Potential Benefits of Including Program Theory Evaluation in Meta-Analysis

*Anthony Petrosino*

Determining whether and why a program has worked is risky business. A randomized experiment—if implemented and conducted with full integrity—can provide the least ambiguous answer to the question, Did the program work? But unless additional data, besides the outcome measures, are planned for and analyzed, an experiment can rarely provide an answer to the question, Why did the intervention work?[1] Even if we could successfully design a study that answers both *whether* and *why* questions, no small feat in itself, there is another problem. Single, stand-alone evaluations will rarely be definitive. Results from evaluations of the same program often vary across settings because of differences in clients, staff, and so on (Lipsey, 1997).

Two different perspectives, however, have emerged that together may provide better answers to whether and why questions. The first is program theory. For at least thirty years, evaluators have written persuasively—and often—about the need to explicitly test program theory in evaluation (for example, Bickman, 1987; Chen and Rossi, 1992; Weiss, 1972). Although the lexicon varies across

*Note:* Earlier drafts of this chapter were presented to the Harvard Children's Initiative Evaluation Task Force (April 1998) and the American Evaluation Association (November 1998). A Spencer Foundation fellowship at the Harvard Children's Initiative and a Mellon Foundation grant to the Center for Evaluation facilitated this work. I appreciate the comments of Mary Askew, Anne Barten, Leonard Bickman, Iain Chalmers, Jodi Delibertis, Timothy Hacsi, Tracy Huebner, Mark Lipsey, Heather McMillan, Frederick Mosteller, Pamela Perry, Carolyn Petrosino, Patricia Rogers, Sean Riordan, Robert Rosenthal, Carol Weiss, and Stuart Yeh. The thoughts expressed herein, however, are those of the author only.

these writers, all agree that evaluations, whenever possible, should articulate and test the underlying assumptions about why the program should "work." For consistency with other chapters in this volume, I adopt the term *program theory evaluation* (PTE) to describe studies using terminology such as *theory-based* or *theory-driven* to describe similar approaches.[2]

The interest in PTE runs parallel to the advent of a science of reviewing. Although attention to the problem of interpreting separate but similar studies dates back to 1904, the science of reviewing took hold in the 1970s with *meta-analysis* (Hunt, 1997). Because it was recognized that traditional methods for synthesizing research were flawed, meta-analysis surfaced as a rigorous method for summarizing the results of prior research (for example, Lipsey, 1990). In contrast to the use of PTE, the use of meta-analysis has been widespread; Lipsey and Wilson (1993) were able to identify over three hundred meta-analyses of social and educational treatment.

Writers such as Cordray (1992) and Lipsey (1997) suggest that the combination of PTE and meta-analysis could have benefits. For example, Lipsey showed how they could be used mutually to build social intervention theories. In this chapter, I build on these earlier arguments to demonstrate how the accumulation of knowledge from PTEs through meta-analysis could provide beneficial data for social policy and practice decisions. Hypothetical illustrations are relied on, as good examples of synthesizing PTEs in meta-analysis have yet to be reported.

## The One-Step Evaluation Model

Many evaluations test only for an intervention's effects on outcome measures—sometimes referred to as one-step models (Weiss, 1997). The problem with the one-step model is that it does not explain why a program should affect the outcome (Chen and Rossi, 1992). It does not address the causal complexity involved in many programs that target outcomes such as criminal behavior. Some social interventions work through indirect processes: a treatment is delivered in one setting and is expected to engage other critical mechanisms in order to affect the outcome in a different setting (Donaldson, forthcoming). For example, school-based drug prevention targets adolescent drug use, presumably by engaging mechanisms such as peer resistance. These mechanisms are supposed to increase resilience to using drugs both inside and outside the schoolyard. The one-step model would ignore the measurement of underlying mechanisms such as peer resistance and would focus only on outcomes such as drug use.

## How One-Step Evaluations Affect Meta-Analysis

The choice to conduct one-step evaluations has ramifications for research synthesis, as the original studies provide the data for meta-analysis. It is important for evaluators to see that how they conduct and report their studies because how they do so influences subsequent reviews.

**Table 6.1. Hypothetical Meta-Analysis of One-Step Evaluations, Sex Offender Treatment**

| Program (N) | Effect on Sex Offense Recidivism | BESD |
|---|---|---|
| Cognitive-based (11) | .30 | +15.00% |
| Behavioral (10) | .11 | +5.50% |
| Individualized (12) | .01 | +.05% |
| Group counseling (8) | −.05 | −2.50% |

Note: Ranked by effect size.

In most meta-analyses, reviewers create an effect size to express the impact of the program on the outcome measure of interest. For example, in an Illinois evaluation, ninety-four juvenile delinquents were randomly assigned to attend a prison tour; sixty-seven youngsters received no contact at all (Greater Egypt Regional Planning & Development Commission, 1979). The program also consisted of an interactive rap session with inmates, who provided the juveniles with realistic stories of prison life, including rape and murder. The "Scared Straight" type program was designed to deter juvenile delinquents from further delinquency. At six months, the evaluators found that 17 percent of the experimental group had been rearrested, compared with 12 percent of the controls, for an effect size of -14.[3] A negative sign is used because the program effect was in the opposite direction anticipated.

In most meta-analyses, effect sizes like these are averaged across all studies (for example, "programs to reduce delinquency had an average effect size of .10"). In some meta-analyses, they are averaged for specific treatments, using broad labels (for example, "vocational programs to reduce delinquency had an average effect size of .05"). Such a label serves two purposes: it provides a title to describe the basic intervention, but it is broad enough to capture more than just a few studies. These categories have implications for meta-analysis. For example, cognitive therapy, behavioral therapy, individualized counseling, and group counseling are all treatments for sex offenders (Laws, 1989). If evaluations of these treatments have been reported, meta-analysis can proceed and effect sizes computed. Most meta-analysts set as a criterion for eligibility that evaluations include either a control or comparison group.

Table 6.1 provides hypothetical results for a meta-analysis of sex offender treatment studies. The table indicates that the effect size for cognitive treatment was .30. Would such a finding be important? Rosenthal and Rubin (1982) provide a way of translating effect sizes into percentage differences, known as the binomial effect size display (BESD). Using BESD, an effect size of .30 translates into a 15 percent improvement for the cognitive group compared with controls. An average 15 percent reduction in sex offender recidivism would be important.[4]

But the broad label of cognitive treatment masks useful information about the programs in that category. There are many different types of cognitive programs for sex offenders, with great variation in how even a single type of program is implemented across sites. Persons charged with responsibility to fund or implement cognitive programs, however, might not find the results in Table 6.1 useful to their decision making. A number of programs are considered cognitive, and the broad label does not indicate which of the cognitive programs they should employ.

## How PTEs Could Be Exploited in Meta-Analysis

One way to overcome this problem is to increase the number of PTEs eligible for meta-analysis. The end of this chapter provides one practical suggestion on how to do this. But even simple PTEs that focus on a single key mechanism and the outcome would provide evidence that programs were working through one particular mechanism or another. Meta-analytical findings could then be categorized by the key mechanism tested in original evaluations. If such mechanisms were tested across a number of PTEs, meta-analysis would be better suited to offering clues for effective intervention.

Returning to Table 6.1, the findings showed that cognitive programs were the most effective strategy for reducing recidivism. But no information on why cognitive programs were more effective was provided. Even more problematic is that the average effect size probably includes programs with a wide range of effects; some were likely very effective, but some likely had smaller effects on recidivism than even noncognitive treatments (for example, group counseling).

Instead of the ten evaluations of cognitive treatment reported in Table 6.1, what if a larger number of simple PTEs were included in the meta-analysis? A simple PTE is what Lipsey and Pollard (1989) describe as a two-step model—the measurement and testing of at least one mechanism for change and one outcome. In applying such a model to evaluations of treatment programs for sex offenders, the design would test whether the program first changed something to subsequently affect recidivism (see Table 6.2).

In Table 6.2, the results from Table 6.1 are compared with a hypothetical meta-analysis of a series of simple PTEs. The advantage of the PTE meta-analysis is that clues about mechanisms for change are provided. Effective programs are more easily identified by the key mechanism they engage. In Table 6.2, for example, cognitive programs that increase the skills of sex offenders to identify and reduce their own high-risk situations are more effective in reducing recidivism. Cognitive programs, if they are to be employed, are even more effective when used in combination with targeting offender empathy. Such findings would be very useful in providing guidance for decision making.

**Table 6.2.  Comparing Hypothetical Meta-Analysis of One-Step Evaluations with Hypothetical Meta-Analysis of PTEs**

*Using One-Step Evaluations*

| Programs (N) Recidivism | Sex Offense Recidivism |
|---|---|
| Cognitive-based (11) | .30 |
| Behavioral (10) | .11 |
| Individualized (12) | .01 |
| Group counseling (8) | −.05 |

*Using Simple PTEs*

| Cognitive-Based Programs (N) | Effect on Mechanism | Sex Offense Recidivism |
|---|---|---|
| Skills in victim empathy (7) | .61 | .44 |
| Skills in high-risk situations (14) | .55 | .38 |
| Reduction in rationalization (8) | .28 | .12 |
| Increase in empathy for victims (12) | .25 | .09 |

## Minimum Requirements of PTEs for Meta-Analysis

For PTEs to be exploited in meta-analysis, they should meet three criteria—an explicit causal model on how the program will affect outcomes, the testing of at least one underlying mechanism as an intervening variable along with outcomes, and control-group data reported for both variables. The first criterion requires a prospective and explicit model to be tested in the evaluation. Not only does the explicitness reduce the amount of guessing that the reader has to do about what the program theory was, but the prospective requirement prevents post hoc fitting of models to data.[5]

The second criterion requires that the PTE include at least one *mediator.* In evaluation terms, the mediator is something that the program must affect or change in order to positively influence the main outcome (Lipsey and Pollard, 1989). Some evaluations that have included program theory did not attempt to test any key links or mechanisms in the model (Petrosino, 2000). Even if a program theory is explicit, if only the outcome data are analyzed and reported, such evaluations provide no more information than one-step models; the program's causal theory was not tested. According to the third criterion, the control or comparison data must be reported for both the mediating and outcome variables. If data on the mediator are reported only for the treatment group, the evaluation provides little evidence that the effect on the mediator would have occurred without the program (see Cook, Chapter Three).

Process-outcome evaluations also do not meet the minimum requirement for PTE, as they provide no data on underlying mechanisms. Even when evaluators link the process data to outcomes in their analyses, these reflect the impact of program activities and the degree of fidelity on outcomes—not the underlying theory of change (Weiss, 1997). Something about these activities should engage a critical mechanism. What is that *something*? That is what PTE must articulate and test (see Weiss, Chapter Four).

## How Could Meta-Analysis of PTEs Inform Larger Social Theories?

In PTE, theory is an explanation about how the program will cause the intended outcomes. Larger scientific theories offer general explanations of phenomena such as criminality, poor learning, or even how programs are implemented. A meta-analysis of PTEs could potentially inform such larger theories.

For example, in Chandler's (1973) experimental evaluation of a role-modeling intervention with troubled youth, he tested a two-step model: reducing egocentrism (that is, lack of empathy for others) would reduce delinquency (Lipsey and Pollard, 1989). Chandler conducted a two-year follow-up and found that treatment achieved statistically significant reductions in both egocentrism and delinquency.

Instead of just one experiment, Table 6.3 provides a hypothetical example of how fifty studies like Chandler's could inform delinquency theory. In Table 6.3, ten PTEs test the egocentrism model; four other groups of PTEs test different mechanisms for change. The table provides hypothetical effect sizes for each of the five categories. Interventions that targeted egocentrism hypothetically achieved the largest effects on both the mediator and subsequent delinquency. Such a finding suggests that a crucial link in the pathogenesis of delinquency is egocentrism.

The hypothetical findings also show that interventions generally had smaller effects on measures of self-esteem, job skills, intrafamily functioning, and fear of sanctioning. Such findings could lead delinquency theorists to reexamine the relationship between such factors and subsequent delinquency. Certainly, the effects could be due to poor program implementation or a generally ineffective treatment (if the ten studies were based on one common treatment type). But all things being equal, a generation of PTEs for meta-analysis could provide some guidance, particularly about problems like delinquency.

**Minimum Threshold Levels and Cascading Effects.** If program theory were well developed for a widespread intervention, PTE data could be exploited in meta-analysis to provide information for decision makers. For example, mediating and outcome variables could permit estimates of minimum threshold levels—the required improvement needed on the mediator to result in improved outcomes. This could be helpful to programs in which the mediators are measured at some point before the outcomes. Failure to achieve a mediating effect could serve as a red flag for decision makers that the program is en route to poor outcomes (Weiss, 1997).

**Table 6.3. Hypothetical Effect Sizes for Mediating and Outcome Variables**

| Mediator (N) | Mediator Effect | Delinquency Effect |
|---|---|---|
| Egocentrism (10) | .64 | .34 |
| Self-esteem (10) | .48 | −.07 |
| Intrafamily functioning (10) | .36 | .17 |
| Job skill enhancement (10) | .22 | .02 |
| Fear of legal sanctioning (10) | .12 | −.15 |

Note: Ranked by mediator effect.

Such data could also portray *cascading effects.*[6] With each subsequent mediating variable in certain program theories, smaller effects will likely be reported. For example, in knowledge-attitude-behavior models (Lipsey, 1997), programs that report large effects on knowledge usually report much smaller effects on the later attitudinal and behavioral measures. Data on cascading effects could be used to signal decision makers that a program needs to be retooled in order to achieve larger effects at later stages. Or maybe the model must be revised to account for other intervening variables.

**The Value-Added of PTE.** Meta-analysis could provide a method for assessing the *value-added* by PTE. Value-added often means something that can be measured mathematically, but here it refers to whether or not PTE provides some benefit beyond other approaches to evaluation. Although the benefits of PTE have long been suggested, they have not been empirically demonstrated. One way to test for value-added is through meta-analysis. For example, Lipton (1995) and his colleagues are conducting a meta-analysis of correctional program evaluations reported since 1968. Their meta-analysis will likely include over a thousand evaluations, some using different approaches such as PTE.

Their data could be used to compare PTE with these other evaluation approaches; the evaluations may not be easily categorized but could be rated along a continuum of how well developed the theory is that is used to guide the evaluation (Lipsey, 1988). The ratings could be analyzed to determine the influence of theory development in PTE on a number of dependent variables, including effect size, program success or failure, and so on. A small sample of the studies could be studied to determine how they were used in subsequent decisions. The data, though suggestive, could provide clues as to the real benefits that PTE provides over process-outcome or one-step model evaluations.

## Barriers and Limitations

Few writers would argue against the inclusion of mediators in an evaluation design (see Cook, Chapter Three, for further discussion). But just as there are barriers in conducting a single PTE, there are roadblocks to using PTEs in meta-analysis. Some of them are outlined in the following discussion.

**The Low Number of PTEs.** The major barrier is the low number of available PTEs reported in the literature. Our own search for good examples of PTE was protracted and painful (see Rogers, Chapter Five, and others in this issue). Even simple PTEs requiring a two-step model are difficult to find; rarely do evaluators explicitly and prospectively articulate a model to be tested.

**Emphasis on Experiments and Quasi-Experiments.** Most meta-analyses require as an eligibility criterion that original evaluations include a control or comparison group. This is a trade-off, increasing internal validity but excluding potentially useful studies that take different methodological approaches to evaluate programs.

**Poor Reporting.** Reviewers are universally unhappy about the quality of reporting in original research documents. The combination of PTE and meta-analysis would require more data to be collected, analyzed, and reported by evaluators. Improving the quality of reporting is something that everyone recommends, but finding solutions has been difficult.

**Simplistic Program Theories.** This chapter has not taken into account complex models. The simple PTEs discussed here are linear and assume a domino effect: a change in one variable will result in a subsequent change in the next measured variable. As Rogers notes (Chapter Five), the world may not operate the way these models suggest. Even in linear theories, models can be lengthy. Weiss (1997) lists seventeen links in her job-training example. As she notes about evaluators doing original studies (Chapter Four), meta-analysts may also be forced to determine which links in which theory to code and examine in reviews.

## One Recommendation for Promoting PTEs

As mentioned earlier, the major barrier to this approach is the lack of PTEs. Sherman and his colleagues (1997) suggest a method for increasing high-quality evaluations. In their review of crime prevention studies for the United States Congress, they also examined evaluation requirements set by the federal and state governments when they fund criminal justice–related programs. Although every grant recipient is usually required as a condition of funding to conduct an evaluation, Sherman and his colleagues found that few are reported. One problem is that what passes for evaluation is sometimes no more than the input data or information on clients served. Of those few outcome or impact studies that are conducted, control or comparison group designs are rarely implemented. The end result is that very little is known about what works in crime prevention, despite the billions of dollars spent over the past two decades (Sherman and others, 1997). One contributing factor is the generally inadequate amount of money allocated to evaluation within the program budget. Sherman and colleagues suggest a different approach: instead of requiring evaluation for every funded program, the administrative agency (usually at the federal or state level) should pool the evaluation monies together to support a small number of high-quality evaluations in just a few sites. Such an approach could help promote an increase in the number of rigorously controlled PTEs.

An example of how this strategy would work in practice is provided by one federal funding program.[7] The Title V Grants for Local Delinquency Prevention Programs from the Office of Juvenile Justice and Delinquency Prevention supported 477 distinct interventions in the United States during fiscal years 1994–1997 (Office of Juvenile Justice and Delinquency Prevention, 1998). Instead of requiring an evaluation at all 477 sites (generally budgeted at $10,000 per site), the $4.7 million earmarked for evaluation could be spent funding PTEs at 20 sites. Each of the PTEs would include random assignment to conditions or reasonably valid comparison groups. Each evaluation would receive $200,000 per site (for a total cost of $4 million). The other monies ($700,000) could be used to build in some limited data collection to monitor non-PTE sites. Following this approach, a meta-analysis of the 20 PTEs could be conducted in a reasonably short time. A systematic and rigorously performed review of 20 PTEs would certainly yield much better information than the 477 low-quality and scattered evaluations that inevitably would be reported.

## Conclusion

The short history of meta-analysis indicates that it has the potential to be both informative and influential (Hunt, 1997). Meta-analysis also means that many evaluations will be utilized by reviewers for years—and will have influence beyond the original jurisdiction in which they were conducted (Lipsey, 1997). Given the eternal "shelf life" of some evaluations because of meta-analysis, evaluators could greatly contribute to the knowledge base by conducting even simple PTEs.

Meta-analysis will take on even greater importance in light of a new international organization, known as the Campbell Collaboration, created in 1999 to facilitate the preparation of systematic, updated, and multinational reviews of social program evaluations (Davies, Petrosino, and Chalmers, 1999). Named after Donald Campbell and modeled after its older sibling in health care (the Cochrane Collaboration), the Campbell Collaboration will also explore methods for improving the precision and validity of both original evaluations and subsequent meta-analysis (its Web site is http://campbell.gse.upenn.edu).

One way to improve meta-analysis is to incorporate more PTEs, providing reviewers with data on mechanisms that could be exploited. In this chapter, four potential benefits for the use of PTE data in meta-analysis have been suggested. Such a happy marriage of these two perspectives would produce an offspring of much better evidence to guide decision making.

## Notes

1. Some may argue that factorial experiments isolate mechanisms for why a program works.
2. I prefer the term *causal model* because of the general confusion surrounding "theory" (Petrosino, 2000).
3. Lipsey (1990) provides a conversion formula for effect sizes.
4. Rosenthal and Rubin's (1982) BESD can convert effect sizes into percentage differences, permitting communication of results to nonacademic audiences.
5. Some evaluations collect considerable data on participants, and some information could be conceptualized as mediating variables. Meta-analysis can handle such "kitchen sink" evaluations—if there are enough of them—and can examine correlations for both mediators and outcome measures.
6. Mark Lipsey suggested the term *cascading effects* (personal communication with author, April 1998).
7. Agencies usually administer grants under different funding "streams." For example, the U.S. Department of Justice has many streams of funding (such as the Violence Against Women Act). Block grants are made to states for each stream, and states then make subgrant awards (Sherman and others, 1997).

## References

Bickman, L. (ed.) *Using Program Theory in Evaluation.* New Directions for Program Evaluation, no. 33. San Francisco: Jossey-Bass, 1987.

Chandler, M. J. "Egocentrism and Antisocial Behavior: The Assessment and Training of Social Perspective-Taking Skills." *Developmental Psychology,* 1973, 9(3), 326–332.

Chen, H. T., and Rossi, P. H. (eds.). *Using Theory to Improve Program and Policy Evaluations.* Westport, Conn.: Greenwood Press, 1992.

Cordray, D. S. "Theory-Driven Meta-Analysis: Practices and Prospects." In H. T. Chen and P. H. Rossi (eds.), *Using Theory to Improve Program and Policy Evaluations.* Westport, Conn.: Greenwood Press, 1992.

Davies, P., Petrosino, A., and Chalmers, I. "The Effects of Social and Educational Interventions: Developing an Infrastructure for International Collaboration to Prepare, Maintain, and Promote the Accessibility of Systematic Reviews of Relevant Research." In *Proceedings of the international meeting on Systematic Reviews of the Effects of Social and Educational Interventions,* London, July 15–16, 1999. Donaldson, S. I. "Mediator and Moderator Analysis in Program Development." In S. Sussman (ed.), *Handbook of Program Development in Health Behavior Research and Practice,* forthcoming. Thousand Oaks, Calif.: Sage.

Greater Egypt Regional Planning & Development Commission. *Menard Correctional Center. Juvenile Tours Impact Study.* Carbondale, Ill.: Greater Egypt Regional Planning & Development Commission, 1979.

Hunt, M. *The Story of Meta-Analysis.* New York: Russell Sage Foundation, 1997.

Laws, R. E. *Relapse Prevention with Sex Offenders.* New York: Guilford Press, 1989.

Lipsey, M. W. "Practice and Malpractice in Evaluation Research." *Evaluation Practice,* 1988, 9(4), 5–24.

Lipsey, M. W. *Design Sensitivity: Statistical Power for Experimental Research.* Thousand Oaks, Calif.: Sage, 1990.

Lipsey, M. W. "What Can You Build with Thousands Of Bricks? Musings on the Cumulation of Knowledge in Program Evaluation." In D. J. Rog and D. Fournier (eds.), *Progress and Future Directions in Evaluation: Perspectives on Theory, Practice, and Methods.* New Directions for Evaluation, no 76. San Francisco: Jossey-Bass, 1997.

Lipsey, M. W., and Pollard, J. A. "Driving Toward Theory in Program Evaluation: More Models to Choose From." *Evaluation and Program Planning,* 1989, 12, 317–328.

Lipsey, M. W., and Wilson, D. "The Efficacy of Psychological, Educational and Behavioral Treatment: Confirmation from Meta-Analysis." *American Psychologist,* 1993, 48(12), 1181–1209.

Lipton, D. S. "Correctional Drug Abuse Treatment Effectiveness: Updating the Effectiveness of Correctional Treatment 25 Years Later." *Journal of Offender Rehabilitation,* 1995, 22, 1–20.

Office of Juvenile Justice and Delinquency Prevention. *1998 Report to Congress: Title V Incentive Grants for Local Delinquency Prevention Programs.* Washington, D.C.: Office of Juvenile Justice and Delinquency Prevention, 1998.

Petrosino, A. "Answering the Why Question in Evaluation: The Causal-Model Approach." *Canadian Journal of Program Evaluation,* 2000, 12(1), 1–25.

Rosenthal, R., and Rubin, D. "A Simple, General Purpose Display of Magnitude of Experimental Effect." *Journal of Educational Psychology,* 1982, 74, 166–169.

Sherman, L. W., and others. *Preventing Crime: What Works, What Doesn't, What's Promising: A Report to the United States Congress.* College Park: Department of Criminology and Criminal Justice, University of Maryland, 1997.

Weiss, C. H. *Evaluation Research: Methods of Assessing Program Effectiveness.* Englewood Cliffs, N.J.: Prentice Hall, 1972.

Weiss, C. H. "Theory-Based Evaluation: Past, Present, and Future." In D. J. Rog and D. Fournier (eds.), *Progress and Future Directions in Evaluation: Perspectives on Theory, Practice, and Methods.* New Directions for Evaluation, no. 76. San Francisco: Jossey-Bass, 1997.

*ANTHONY PETROSINO is research fellow at the Center for Evaluation, Initiatives for Children Program, American Academy of Arts and Sciences and research associate at the Harvard Graduate School of Education.*

7

*Program theory evaluation can provide the kind of detailed information about what aspects of a program lead to success that is needed to replicate programs in new and varied settings.*

# Using Program Theory to Replicate Successful Programs

*Timothy A. Hacsi*

One of the greatest problems faced by policymakers and program managers concerned with ongoing social problems—for example, juvenile delinquency or drug abuse—is developing effective programs. When a program seems to be successful, replicating that program effectively turns out to be even more difficult. Many programs have multiplied because of an obvious social need, or political decisions, or shrewd marketing, rather than because of real evidence that they are effective; such programs generally do not work well. To make matters worse, true believers often claim that the evidence is on their side, whether it is or not. One of the reasons they are able to do this is that the available evaluation evidence on many issues is cloudy and can be interpreted in multiple ways (Hacsi, forthcoming). Perhaps if evidence were available about which programs worked well that also explained *why* effective programs were effective, it would be more likely to influence policymakers. Such detailed evidence would certainly be of use to program managers striving to make a difference. It is therefore not going too far out on a limb to suggest that providing detailed, specific knowledge about what aspects of a successful program make it successful should be, at times, a goal of evaluation. If this is true for social programs, it is also true in general for the vast array of areas where evaluators work.

For an evaluator, one common goal is to determine whether or not the program being evaluated is successful. In many cases, randomized experiments are the proper approach because they are the best way to prove what a program's results actually were. But randomized experiments usually do not show what it was about the program that led to its outcomes. The more complex the program, the more difficult it is to know just what the treatment actually entailed. Was it the curriculum, or the charismatic program manager, or the relationships between clients and program staff, or a particular combination of these and other factors that led to success in the original program? Most randomized experiments have little to say about these components.

## Replication and Adaptation

Programs that are viewed as successful or admirable are replicated in various ways. Sometimes a program will be replicated in another, similar, setting; it then exists in two places, and there are almost guaranteed to be differences, both intentional and unintentional, between how the two programs function. Another common way for a program to become widespread is through government or foundation action, when a program that exists in at most a few locales is suddenly scaled up into dozens, or hundreds, of settings. This kind of widespread diffusion rarely has positive outcomes (Shadish, Cook, and Leviton, 1991).

Given the importance and variability of local actors and specific environments in how a social program functions, complete replication is probably not a feasible or desirable goal in most cases, whether done one at a time or as a broad diffusion across numerous sites. What is actually needed is information that will enhance the likelihood of *adapting* a model program to circumstances in different locales. The more a new setting (staff, clientele, and so forth) differs from a successful program's original locale, the more the program may have to be changed to succeed in that new setting. I argue in the following discussion that program theory evaluation (PTE) has the potential to provide knowledge about what parts of a program must be retained and what parts can be changed, or even abandoned. The discussion may also be able to give some guidance concerning how a program would need to be changed to function in a new and notably different environment. If PTE can do this, it will provide information crucial to successful adaptation of a program into new settings, thus making it easier to "scale up" good programs for wider use.

## Different Approaches to Replication

Scholars outside of evaluation bring a variety of approaches to the idea of scaling up successful programs. I will briefly describe arguments by two such thinkers, Lisbeth Schorr and Richard Elmore. Over the past two decades, Schorr has studied a number of programs that seem to be "breaking the cycle of disadvantage" for high-risk children. She has tried to distill the attributes that these programs have in common in the belief that doing so will enhance the diffusion of effective programs. Schorr argues that successful programs for at-risk children offer a broad spectrum of services, are flexible, are coherent and easy to use, and so on (Schorr, 1988). Schorr has also developed eight strategies to guide attempts to scale up, such as abandoning the idea of a "single fix" for poverty and getting all pertinent stakeholders on the same page (Schorr, 1997).

Unfortunately, Schorr's findings are of limited help in actually planning how to replicate or adapt any specific program. For one thing, there are undoubtedly programs that are successful even though they do not contain each of the attributes Schorr lists. More fundamentally, Schorr's approach does little to describe the day-to-day practices and the ongoing contacts between program staff and clientele that may be necessary for the adaptation of successful programs in new settings. Her list of attributes and strategies are useful to bear in mind, but they are far too general to be of much help to program managers trying to develop and implement a program. Schorr provides a list of descriptions that will fit (more or less) most successful social programs but does not provide any way to get at the details that go to the heart of a successful program.

Along somewhat similar lines, Elmore (1996) considers the difficulty of replicating educational success on a large scale. Elmore argues, quite rightly, that successful educational reforms occur regularly in individual classrooms, schools, and even school systems. He believes that they fail to spread widely because the incentive structures of schools make it extremely difficult to change what he calls the *core* of educational practice—student roles in learning and teacher assumptions about the nature of knowledge and its transmission. Elmore goes on to make a number of insightful arguments about what must change for meaningful educational reform to spread. He makes a sophisticated argument about how to make schools more amenable to replicating success, but his approach does not describe how to replicate any specific success. It would provide a better environment for reform (though in fact such reforms could be good or bad, useful or harmful) but would not shape specific reforms. This is of course important, as are Schorr's ideas. The question remains, however, When trying to take successful program A into locations B and C, what do you do?.

## A Historian's Brief Take on Cause and Effect

Before trying to answer that question, a few words about how we "know" a program works—about cause and effect in evaluation—are in order. The idea that PTE can provide real information about which aspects of a program have a specific effect on eventual outcomes implies that PTE can develop causal knowledge. Some evaluators believe that the only way to develop meaningful causal knowledge is through randomized experiments, or at the least through quasi-experimental methods and extensive use of statistics. I do not necessarily agree, and others also have doubts (see Davidson, Chapter Two; Maxwell, 1996).

I was trained as a historian, and historians develop cause-and-effect arguments without anything resembling experimental or quasi-experimental methods. The issues that historians study are at least as complex as any program, and one major goal of historians is to understand how numerous actors, social forces, and ideas interacted to lead to certain events or developments. They do so through an ongoing search for evidence—comparisons of dozens, hundreds, or even thousands of different sources—and a continual testing of multiple hypotheses. A historian's results can be, at times, as convincing as the findings of most randomized experiments. To be sure, historical causal explanations are less certain than the kind of knowledge developed through good experiments and are never absolute. In this way, a historical causal explanation is noticeably weaker than one achieved by a good randomized experiment. Conversely, historical cause-and-effect explanations can be far more detailed than the results of most randomized experiments, showing how the outcomes were actually reached. It is this sort of nuanced causal knowledge that I believe PTEs can provide. There is, in effect, a trade-off—more knowledge about *why* and *how* something works but less certainty about *how powerfully* it works. This is not always a desirable trade-off, but at times it may be very worthwhile; it is this kind of knowledge that I believe PTEs can sometimes provide and that can help guide more effective diffusion of successful programs into multiple settings.

## What Program Theory Brings to the Table, and One Example

What do I mean by program theory evaluation? Different authors have used different phrases and have meant somewhat different things when they have described *theory-based, theory-driven, logic model,* and other approaches using a program's underlying theory in an evaluation (see Rogers, Chapter Five, and others, this volume). Weiss gives my favorite definition, describing the theory as "the set of beliefs that underlie action. The theory doesn't have to be uniformly accepted. It doesn't have to be right. It is a set of hypotheses upon which people build their program plans" (1998, p. 55). This entails examining the "mechanisms that mediate between the delivery (and receipt) of the program and the emergence of the outcomes of interest" (1998, p. 57). This approach is spreading, but evaluations that actually do employ it in a methodical and thorough manner are still relatively rare. For the purposes of this chapter, what is meant by PTE is broad. It means using the theory (or multiple theories) that describe how a program is supposed to be effective to help develop and guide an evaluation.

Some evaluations have been performed that intentionally or unintentionally used theory to develop the kind of knowledge needed to replicate the program being studied. For example, Ross Homel (1990) describes an evaluation of the deterrent effects of random breath testing (RBT) in New South Wales, Australia, in the 1980s. Extensive RBT was introduced with the goal of reducing drunk driving and road fatalities involving alcohol. The program worked quite well, with an immediate drop in road fatalities of 22 percent, and a reduction of 36 percent in road fatalities and serious injuries involving alcohol. The results were maintained for at least the following four years. To conduct the evaluation, a model was developed of how RBT was supposed to deter drunk driving. The outcome of the evaluation, which relied on interviews and surveys, provided much additional information beyond the simple fact that it had worked. For example, the evaluation showed that informal sanctions through peer pressure played as large a role in reducing drunk driving as did the fear of punishment. In addition, how often an individual's circle of friends had been tested at checkpoints was a powerful predictor of how that individual perceived the likelihood of being tested. And people modified their drinking and driving patterns based on these perceptions. All in all, the model that was being tested seemed to be accurate, and even more important, the evaluation showed *which* links in the model mattered the most. As a result, the evaluation provided knowledge that could be useful for planning related programs in the future (Homel, 1990).

## A Hypothetical Addition to Project STAR

Cook (Chapter Three) argues that PTE approaches should be used within randomized experiments but not as replacements for them. I agree that randomization, if done well, gives much stronger evidence for causal connections than PTE can provide. The ideal option would be to do as Cook suggests, by using program theory within randomized experiments. Such an evaluation could conceivably show convincingly how well a program worked as well as why and how it worked, all at once. This would be a crucial gain; randomized experiments now rarely achieve nearly so much.

One of the best, and most influential, randomized experiments ever conducted in education was Tennessee's Project STAR (Student/Teacher Achievement Ratio), which examined the effects of smaller classes on student achievement. It showed clearly that children placed in classes of thirteen to seventeen students from kindergarten to third grade did better on standardized tests than did children in classes of twenty-two to twenty-six students (Finn and Achilles, 1990). Follow-up studies have shown that the effects last, as children who had been in the smaller classes continue to score more highly than their counterparts all the way into high school. The federal government and a number of states have funded smaller classes, partly in response to Project STAR's results. They have done so in a variety of ways, usually targeting disadvantaged children, whom STAR shows benefit twice as much from smaller classes as do middle-class children (Hacsi, forthcoming).

But how exactly do smaller classes make a difference? There are many possible explanations. Students might receive more individual attention or have more time to ask questions. It might be easier for teachers to recognize when children are falling behind, or to tailor individual learning plans, or to keep order in the classroom. But we do not know which of these really matter, or if it is some combination of them, or if it is other things altogether. We do not know if the impact of smaller classes will be much greater if teachers use one approach rather than another, for example. As a result, the implementation of smaller classes in some places will be far less effective than it was in Project STAR.

If there had been a PTE component embedded within Project STAR to study *why,* *how,* and *when* class size matters, however, we would know more about what aspects of smaller classes had helped students learn more. Schools and teachers currently implementing smaller classes in the early grades would have more information about how to maximize the impact of this reform than they do now. Given the complex nature of teaching and learning, we might not know much with great certainty, but we would know more than we do now. And the policy implementation of smaller classes might have been done very differently in some places. Some children placed in smaller classes may not benefit at all, particularly in some urban schools in California, because of the way the program has been implemented. This is due largely to politics and not to weaknesses in Project STAR, to be sure; even so, if we knew more about how smaller classes help children learn more effectively, the creation of smaller classes would almost certainly have a much greater impact on students' long-term achievement. PTEs can provide that kind of knowledge.

## Conclusion

I do not mean to argue that PTEs can erase the difficulty of expanding the best social programs, or other kinds of programs, into multiple settings. Some programs work because of idiosyncratic factors, such as a charismatic manager, which cannot be easily replicated or adapted no matter how well we understand them. Political, financial, and other factors will always complicate the spread of any program. Clients are generally interested in knowledge that will help them in the short-term, not in knowledge that might or might not be useful for later replication. In addition, PTEs can be expensive and difficult to conduct. In many cases, they are not appropriate or even necessary. However, as we try to develop good programs and then scale up, PTEs can play an important, and necessary, role. In particular, evaluations of demonstration projects—which are created with the hope of eventually being replicated—should pay close attention to program theory.

Think about the potential of PTEs and educational reform. Over the past fifteen years of extensive educational reform in the United States, a great deal of attention has been paid to charismatic educational leaders. In some cases, successful changes in schools or even entire school systems have been attributed to a specific individual. But is it that person, or that person's methods, or the setting the person entered, or a combination of these and other things that has led to success? At the moment, we do not really know. Some individuals have had remarkable success in one place but when they went elsewhere have failed. Some systemic changes have worked in one place but not in others. PTEs of such reforms would develop a theory (or multiple theories) of *how* school leaders have made a difference and then trace these individuals' actions, their decisions, the setting in which they work, their relations with those around them, and so on. A series of such evaluations would tell us a great deal.

I agree with Cook (Chapter Three) that PTE should be used within randomized experiments, but I have a somewhat different purpose in mind. In specific areas, such as programs to prevent teen pregnancy or adolescent drug use, a handful of randomized PTEs might provide more useful knowledge about what works, how it works, why it works, and for whom it works than dozens of less thorough—and less expensive—evaluations. It is just this kind of knowledge that we need to begin building if we hope to dramatically improve social (and other) programs as a whole. It will allow us to benefit more from the best programs that are developed instead of reinventing the wheel on a daily basis, or replicating ineffective programs, or misunderstanding why a program was effective in the first place.

What exactly should evaluators conducting PTEs focus on to aid better diffusion of good programs? Weiss (Chapter Four) suggests ways to choose specific links to study. I believe, in a related vein, that evaluators interested in promoting better replication should target the basic assumptions of whole categories of programs to learn more about what actually works well and what does not. For example, many prevention programs for children and adolescents are based on the knowledge-attitude-behavior plan—provide knowledge, which will change attitude, which in turn will lead to changed behavior. Individuals who can remember what motivated them when they were adolescents will recognize that this is a problematic strategy. If a number of PTEs were conducted on prevention programs, focusing on one or more of these critical junctures, together they might reveal what conjunction of circumstances, activities, and clientele lead to better results at each step of the way. Similarly, in other areas, PTEs that focus on the fundamental aspects of a type of program could lead to a body of knowledge that would greatly increase our ability to learn from, and replicate, successful programs. Program theory evaluation is not a panacea for the problem of replicating the best programs into wider use. But it can make a significant contribution to efforts to do so, and any step forward on this issue would be worth taking.

## References

Elmore, R. F. "Getting to Scale with Good Educational Practice." *Harvard Educational Review*, 1996, 66(1), 1–26.

Finn, J. D., and Achilles, C. M. "Answers and Questions About Class Size: A Statewide Experiment." *American Educational Research Journal*, 1990, 27(3), 557–577.

Hacsi, T. A. *Schools and the Evidence: Education Policy-Making and Evaluation.* Cambridge: Harvard University Press, forthcoming.

Homel, R. "Random Breath Testing in New South Wales: The Evaluation of a Successful Social Experiment." *National Evaluation Conference 1990, Proceedings*, vol. 1. Australasian Evaluation Society, 1990.

Maxwell, J. A. *Using Qualitative Research to Develop Causal Explanations.* Cambridge, Mass.: Harvard Project on Schooling and Children Working Paper, 1996.

Schorr, L. B. *Common Purpose: Strengthening Families and Neighborhoods to Rebuild America.* New York: Anchor Books, 1997.

Schorr, L. B., with Schorr, D. *Within Our Reach: Breaking the Cycle of Disadvantage.* New York: Anchor Books, 1988.

Shadish, W. R., Jr., Cook, T. D., and Leviton, L. C. *Foundations of Program Evaluation: Theories of Practice.* Thousand Oaks, Calif.: Sage, 1991.

Weiss, C. H. *Evaluation: Methods for Studying Programs and Policies.* (2d ed.) Englewood Cliffs, N.J.: Prentice Hall, 1998.

*TIMOTHY A. HACSI is research fellow at the Harvard Children's Initiative and teaches history at the Harvard Extension School.*

*This chapter explores how theory-based evaluation can be used to help conduct formative, reflective evaluations in educational settings.*

# Theory-Based Evaluation: Gaining a Shared Understanding Between School Staff and Evaluators

*Tracy A. Huebner*

Gaining cooperation from program staff is an ongoing problem for evaluators. This is true in schools and in a number of other settings. This chapter focuses on how theory-based evaluation can help address this problem in school evaluations, but its argument applies to a broad array of evaluations.

Five significant challenges plague school site evaluations. One of the barriers is staff's lack of receptivity to an outsider coming in to evaluate their programs. There are several reasons for this lack of receptivity. For example, teachers may have had negative experiences with evaluators in the past; evaluations may have led to the closing of a program. Or teachers may have felt that they were misrepresented in a final analysis. Whatever the reason, teachers unwilling to participate in an evaluation make the task difficult.

A second challenge for evaluators is that teachers are not trained in evaluation. Because they may not see or understand the relevance of this work to their own, they may be less than willing to participate in data collection or other aspects of an evaluation. For example, the teacher at Woodland who told an evaluator to do his job while she did hers did not understand her role in the evaluation. This is not unusual. Teachers often

*Note:* Earlier drafts of this chapter were presented to the Evaluation Task Force of the Harvard Children's Initiative and the American Evaluation Association Annual Conference in 1998. This chapter was generously sponsored by a grant from the Spencer Foundation. The author wishes to acknowledge the wonderful insights and support of Carol Weiss, Timothy Hacsi, Anthony Petrosino, Patricia Rogers, Barbara Neufeld, and George Madaus.

perceive the role of evaluation as outside of their arena; anything having to do with evaluation has nothing to do with them. Compounded with the challenges of teacher resistance and lack of training, evaluators are also burdened with the difficulties of evaluating complex school-based programs.

Third, schools have weak veins of communication. Oftentimes messages sent from the administration to the teachers about a new program or policy are interpreted in as many different ways as there are teachers. Because administrators spend so little time in classrooms, and teachers spend the majority of their time teaching independently, there is no method in place to clarify these different interpretations. Instead the separation between administrator and teacher exacerbates the communication problem.

Fourth, adding to the challenge of an already weakened system of communication is the fact that school-based programs are very complex. Many of the current school reform efforts combine both administrative and academic change (see, for example, the Accelerated Schools Project and the Coalition for Essential Schools).[1] Programs are asking teachers to change not only the way they teach but also the way they participate in the school community, for example, participating in school governance boards and interacting with the parents and business community. This means that the evaluator has to look at not only the academic development of students but also the culture and climate of the school. All components are intertwined, and disentangling them is a challenge. Communication and complexity are two issues that are difficult to handle but can be addressed by evaluators.

A fifth challenge beyond the boundary of control of evaluators is the fact that many programs are not in place long enough for us to really learn about their merits and weaknesses. All too often, programs are terminated after one or two years of operation based on the claim that student test scores did not increase. But research on school change tells us that it takes at least five years to observe substantive change (Fullan, 1991).

With all of these challenges in front of evaluators, how are we working to address them? Evaluators are turning to innovative approaches to involve educators more directly in the evaluation process. They are drawing on different models of evaluation to break down barriers between teachers and administrators, as well as between school staff and themselves.

Theory-based evaluation is one model that attempts to include program staff in the design and implementation of the evaluation. This model identifies the mechanisms, or the links, between the planned activities and the anticipated outcomes. This chapter explores theory-based evaluation as an approach to conducting formative, reflective evaluations in educational settings. Although the chapter looks specifically at school sites, the lessons learned can be applied to other programs as well. In practice, this model of evaluation helps schools clarify program goals, improve cooperation and buy-in in an evaluation, and encourage reflective practice.

## Empirical Evidence to Support Theory-Based Evaluation with School-Based Programs

Information was gathered through interviews and the study of documents.[2] I examined four theory-based evaluations conducted by four different evaluation teams all adhering to two criteria: each program had an explicit model of its "theory" identified by the evaluator and program staff before the actual evaluation took place, and the evaluation tested at least one mechanism in addition to its ultimate outcome.[3]

I identified three major themes in their evaluations. First, evaluators reported that the process of using logic models as a way to identify the program theory helped both the evaluation team and the school staff clarify program goals. Second, by establishing a common understanding of the program's goals and evaluating the program based on this shared understanding, school staff tended to be more cooperative throughout the course of the evaluation. Third, two evaluators in the sample believed that implementing a theory-based evaluation encouraged teachers to be more reflective in their own practice. (For more about the relationship between theory-based evaluation and reflective practice, see Huebner, 1998.) The matrix depicted in Table 8.1 identifies the evaluators and provides a brief description of each evaluation, the mechanisms tested, and the reported advantages to using the theory-based model. Following the matrix is a more detailed description of the programs and the themes identified in support of theory-based evaluation.

**Helps Clarify Program Goals.** The evaluators reported that theory-based evaluations not only helped establish a rapport between the evaluator and the school staff but also helped unify the staff. The initial process that helped pull all parties together was the activity of developing a logic model of the program's theory. Evaluators reported that the act of designing logic models was perceived as an important step in building relationships with the school staff. Designing these models helped staff feel included in the evaluation, offered evaluators a chance to interact in a nonthreatening way with staff, and acted as an important tool, once they were developed, to help the evaluator and staff identify key questions for evaluation.

Together the staff and evaluator had a shared understanding of how the program was supposed to work at each level. Gaining clarity so that all parties involved in the evaluation were aware of the activities and the mechanisms leading to the intended outcomes was perceived as a critical first step toward a successful evaluation.

Owen and Lambert (1995) believed that their 1993 evaluation of a technology program that had been initiated in a fifth-grade curriculum was enhanced because it had begun with a logic model. The evaluators worked with the staff to define their theory of how the integration of computers would affect the existing curriculum. The model helped "identify the full range of program consequences and, *in addition,* plac[ed] the program within the context of the total school system" (p. 246).

**Table 8.1. Matrix of Four Evaluations Using
a Theory-Based Approach**

| Evaluator | Description of Evaluation | Mechanisms Tested[a] | Reported Advantages to Using a Theory-Based Model |
|---|---|---|---|
| Owen and Lambert (1995) | Evaluate the introduction of laptop computers into a middle-school curriculum. | Links among (1) providing teachers with basic skills related to personal mastery of laptop computers, which (2) helps teachers develop a strong level of proficiency in programming skills, (3) provides more opportunities for students to learn independently at their own pace, and (4) integrates laptop computer use into the classroom. | Unintended outcome had broad implications for school goals—for example, implications for curriculum impact, professional development, and support. |
| Finnan and Davis (1995) | Evaluate the implementation of a whole school reform effort at the whole school and class room levels. | (Individual classroom models were tested only.[b]) Example, links among (1) planning and implementing grade-appropriate material, (2) providing one-on-one instruction for students in need, and (3) assigning at-home reading, which (4) results in increased student reading proficiency. | Teachers became more actively engaged in evaluation—collecting and analyzing data. Teachers reported greater awareness of how their classroom fit in with the overall philosophy and process of the school. |

| | | Mechanisms tested[a] | |
|---|---|---|---|
| Beckford (1998) | Evaluate whether or not intelligence can be learned. | (At this point, only an impact evaluation is being done.) Future links among (1) improving school leadership, which (2) leads to change in teacher attitudes and beliefs, which in turn (3) encourages teachers to use new assessment practices. | Staff grew to understand their program better. |
| Darling (1998) | Evaluate the integration of an eighth-grade core curriculum with state standards. | Links among (1) orienting students in reading, writing, communications, critical thinking, and independent learning, which (2) helps students build schema for understanding history.[c] | Teachers were more actively engaged in evaluation design and implementation. They altered practices as a result of learning from the evaluation. |

[a]*Mechanisms tested* refers to the actual links in the program theory that were tested, therefore this column does not reflect entire program theories.

[b]Actual evaluation was not carried out because the school closed while the evaluation was under way.

[c]Darling reports only the first phase of the evaluation at the time of this chapter.

Owen and Lambert's evaluation linked the technology program with the inner workings of the school as a whole. So instead of just focusing on how the technology program worked in isolation, the theory-based evaluation helped address questions that asked how the program was working *and* how it was working *in the context of* the school's overall organizational structure. For example, did the computer program support the math curriculum? Did it support the overall goals of the school to create an interactive learning environment for children? Owen and Lambert's theory-based evaluation clarified program goals and enabled the evaluators to see how they fit in with the overarching school goals—a very important component for evaluation of school-based programs.

This strategy was also used by Finnan and Davis (1995) in their evaluation of Berry Elementary School's approach to schoolwide reform. They reported that as a result of this approach teachers as well as administrators came together for the first time and worked toward a common understanding of what was happening in classrooms. Together the staff looked at how classroom activities related to what was happening schoolwide. Once this common understanding was established, the faculty and staff worked together with the help of the external evaluators to design an evaluation to meet classroom and schoolwide needs.

Darling and her evaluation team of teachers at Wenatchee Middle School used a theory-based model of evaluation to look at an integrated eighth-grade social studies and language arts curriculum (J. Darling, personal communication with author, Mar.–May 1998). They used the logic model as a way to determine the soundness of their program design as well as to select goals and activities to streamline the curriculum. The process of developing a logic model helped the teachers compare their student achievement goals with outcomes and modify the program according to their needs. In addition, the teachers wanted to use a model that was clear to all stakeholders in the school community. They believed that using a theory-based evaluation would enable them to provide a clear picture of their program and the evaluation to those not directly involved. They wanted this clarity so that other members of the school community would understand their work, understand their evaluation, and critique both.

Ian Beckford (personal communication with author, Mar.–Apr. 1998), like Darling, believed that the process of developing a model of the program's theory helped explain the program more clearly to both himself and the staff, and this clarity in turn helped ensure a more accurate evaluation. Although he talked positively about the process, Beckford was careful to warn of the challenges he had faced in using this model of evaluation. As a result of choosing to work with staff rather than independently, Beckford came up against many interpersonal conflicts regarding the evaluation. His struggle with school staff was not in creating an evaluation based on their program theory as much as it was in developing the model itself. This is not all that uncommon. Weiss (1997) notes that program staff often have difficulty articulating what their theories are.

Beckford's most current work, in 1998, with two educational programs, one a small-scale after school homework-tutoring program and the other a large-scale national school reform effort, involves identifying the program's theory with staff as a way to "work through with [staff] what they [think] the program is about" (Beckford, personal communication with author, 1998). As a result of this time spent "up front," Beckford felt that his clients and program staff with whom he worked were more attuned to the overall development and process of the evaluation.

**Builds Cooperation and Buy-In, Which Helps Develop the Evaluation.** Based on both Darling's and Beckford's observations of developing logic models of program theory, a good way to develop the models is with the assistance of program staff. The evaluator should take the lead role as facilitator. As a result of this common experience, the staff becomes more receptive and willing to participate in the evaluation. In the majority of evaluations reviewed, staff expressed an interest in raising the questions for the evaluation, collecting data for the evaluation, and analyzing the data.

The evaluations reviewed in this chapter include school staff as critical players in the development of these models. After all, who knows the program better than the ones participating in it day to day? In contrast, the evaluator is key in the development of the program theory because it is the evaluator who provides the viewpoint of the outsider—one who can see the forest for the trees (Patton, 1997). These blended perspectives help build a well-rounded picture of the program, its goals, and the mechanisms by which the program seeks to attain them.

Finnan and Davis (1995) wrote about using evaluation to link individual teachers' work with whole school goals and about the powerful connection it helped both teachers and administrators make. They wanted to engage teachers in understanding what was happening in their classrooms as well as in the school as a whole and how the two were interrelated. They also wanted to provide teachers the opportunity to take control and direct their own evaluation by examining the issues that they believed were most relevant to their teaching and their school.

Darling argued that data collection must be "practical, useful, meaningful and trustworthy" in order for members of the school community to find the evaluation credible. She believed that using a theory-based evaluation would help her develop a systematic strategy to meet this end. Her prior experience taught her that "no faculty seems to voluntarily and systematically evaluate their own program. . . . we have no practitioner-designed tools to fulfill our program evaluation responsibility; we have very few (if any) practical, useful, meaningful, trustworthy methods for systematically improving our teaching ourselves" (Darling, personal communication with author, Mar.–May 1998).

However, despite Darling's positive view of the merits of using a theory-based evaluation, the majority of her colleagues were less interested in the actual work of data collection and analysis and more in the development of program models. Teachers were more interested in developing the model than in looking at its implementation. She wrote, "The front end [designing logic models] was really their only interest because basically everything else seems unimportant to them. [Teachers] want to develop and improve programs but are not interested in collecting or analyzing data in the traditional sense. . . . There was little interest in finding out about implementation, more interest was in development of a program, trying to conceptualize it in a practical way" (Darling, personal communication with author, Mar.–May 1998).

Darling's impressions of teachers' reactions to evaluation are grounded in only one experience. It is quite possible that the teachers were less inclined to participate in the evaluation for reasons beyond the scope of what this chapter covers. There is no direct evidence suggesting that the use of a theory-based model of evaluation inhibited or encouraged the teachers from Wenatchee to evaluate their curriculum any more or less than a different model.

Teachers do not often know how a school goes through reform and the role they play in the reform. The theory-based evaluations of Darling and Finnan and Davis helped stress these connections and make teachers aware of how the work they do in their classrooms relates to the overall goals of the department and the school. As a result, both Darling and Finnan and Davis believed that their evaluations received greater support from the teachers than they would have if the teachers had not been involved in the initial planning phase.

**Encourages Reflective Practice.** Another important benefit of a theory-based model is its potential to encourage *reflective practice* in educators. Reflective practice is the process by which teachers actively think about their work and how it affects their students. Based on this understanding, teachers can modify instruction to better meet the learning needs of the students. Teachers exist beyond the landscape of the classroom. A teacher is an individual who works with others to help deepen knowledge. This teaching role—working with others to increase knowledge and understanding—exists in many different sectors, for example, in the health profession when doctors work with residents to train them in their craft. This relationship also exists in community-based programs for youth and adults, where program staff work with clients to increase their knowledge and understanding on any number of issues. As a result of the widespread need for good instructional practice, evaluators must think about the benefit of encouraging reflectivity in general.

Dewey believed that teachers should engage in reflective practice in order to promote opportunities for student learning. He argued that reflective practice is intentional and is directed to the aim of making meaning from interactive teaching episodes. Why encourage reflective practice? Because the act of teaching, whether it is in a classroom or any other context, is a complex act. Reflecting on practice is one way to address myriad intricacies faced by teachers as well as others engaged in working with individuals in a learning capacity. Teachers need to be able to sort through volumes of material in order to teach content to students. It is not enough for teachers to select materials at random for their subject. They must know how to cull and identify the most salient materials that are appropriate for their students and that accurately represent what they are trying to teach. The teachers who reflect thoughtfully about students and subject matter are the teachers who best design methods and materials.

Reflecting on data collected for an evaluation and modifying one's practice to address the needs of the learners is precisely what Schön had in mind when writing not only about reflective practice (1983) but also about his work with Argyris on theory-of-action evaluation (Argyris and Schön, 1974) ten years prior.

In Darling's evaluation, teachers worked together for four days, building their logic model for their eighth-grade social studies curriculum. Darling equated those four days as "four days of reflective practice and for most of us, exhausting and exhilarating." Darling thought that the teachers engaged more in reflection on action than reflection in action. Darling and her colleagues thought that reflection occurred outside the classroom. "When we are actually practicing, life is crazy. We have zero time to reflect. We're just scrambling—trying to get progress reports out, talking to parents, running off papers, tinkering with rooms, etc." (Darling, personal communication with author, Mar.–May 1998).

In Finnan and Davis's evaluation, teachers were encouraged to actively record and think about their practice and its relation to their overall goals both at the classroom level and the whole school level. Teachers engaged in thinking through their own theories of how their students would achieve their ultimate learning goals. Throughout the year, teachers were encouraged to reflect on how their students were progressing academically. Teachers recorded student performance, made observations regarding student work, and modified their practices to better address the needs of their students. In addition, teachers were encouraged to see the links between their own classroom interactions and the school as a whole.

Finnan and Davis's work suggests that involving teachers in an evaluation by encouraging them to look at their own classroom and to see how their work in the classroom affects the overall motion of the school toward reform provides a rich forum for reflection. The evaluators worked with Berry Elementary School to chart the change process at the school sites—the links between and within the classroom, small group, and whole school.

Not all teachers were able to be reflective on their practice and to modify it based on data collected in the evaluation. Some teachers fell into the act of engaging in a process-outcome evaluation. Instead of using student work to reflect on how their presumed mechanisms lead to improved student outcomes, they used the data and journal as a checklist to record their activities. This is not surprising. Not all individuals are predisposed to being reflective. The development of a reflective practitioner is a combination of innate qualities and learned habits (La Boskey, 1994). Teachers predisposed to reflection are more likely to engage in the process of reflecting on their instructional practice and its effects on student learning. For others, reflection is something that they feel they do not have the time for or that it is an act in which they cannot engage without ample coaching.

## Conclusions

This chapter presents data on only four evaluators engaged in theory-based evaluations in educational contexts. Although the initial findings of all four evaluators suggest the benefits of using this strategy, a more substantive investigation is required.

When developed and articulated by both the evaluator and the program staff, program theory provides an approach for mutual understanding of the intentions of the program, and it is a way of laying the groundwork for comprehending why an evaluation is useful and what kind of evaluation design is most beneficial.

Schools seeking to implement evaluations that are helpful to teachers in the classroom and schoolwide may choose to implement a theory-based evaluation. This model moves beyond the black box and provides information about how and why a program functions rather than judging whether or not the program works.

Evaluators using a theory-based evaluation with school-based programs believe that it helps clarify program goals and increase buy-in and participation in the actual evaluations. In addition, theory-based evaluation encourages teachers to be more reflective in their practice. This occurs through the process of collecting data and reflecting on the data, which is a way for teachers to evaluate their practice and their students' learning based on their instruction.

## Notes

1. Information regarding the Accelerated Schools Project can be accessed on line at www.stanford.edu/group/asp/natlcenter.html. For information regarding the Coalition of Essential Schools, refer to www.ces.org.

2. I engaged in personal communication with three of the four evaluation teams, and in two instances I spoke with members who participated in the evaluations, such as teachers and a school principal. In all cases, I talked with the evaluators about the differences they perceived between using a theory-based model of evaluation and another approach. I also talked in depth with the evaluators, teachers, and a principal about the challenges and successes of using logic models as a way to interpret and evaluate a school-based program.

3. The criteria for the definition of theory-based evaluation were determined by Weiss, Hacsi, Huebner, Petrosino, and Rogers in 1998 at the Harvard Children's Initiative.

## References

Argyris, C., and Schön, D. A. *Theory in Practice: Increasing Professional Effectiveness.* San Francisco: Jossey-Bass, 1974.

Finnan, C., and Davis, S. "Linking Project Evaluation and Goals-Based Teacher Evaluation: Evaluating the Accelerated Schools Project in South Carolina." Paper presented at the annual meeting for the American Educational Research Association, San Francisco, 1995.

Fullan, M. *The New Meaning of Educational Change.* (2nd ed.) New York: Teachers College Press, 1991.

Huebner, T. "Theory-Based Evaluation and Reflective Practice: What's the Link?" Unpublished paper, 1998.

La Boskey, V. *Development of Reflective Practice.* New York: Teachers College Press, 1994.

Owen, J., and Lambert, F. "Roles for Evaluation in Learning Organizations." *Evaluation 1,* 1995, *1,* 237–250.

Patton, M. *Utilization-Focused Evaluation.* Thousand Oaks, Calif.: Sage, 1997.

Schön, D. A. *The Reflective Practitioner.* San Francisco: Jossey-Bass, 1983.

Weiss, C. H. "Theory-Based Evaluation: Past, Present, and Future." In D. J. Rog and D. Fournier (eds.), *Progress and Future Directions in Evaluation: Perspectives on Theory, Practice, and Methods.* New Directions for Evaluation, no 76. San Francisco: Jossey-Bass, 1997.

Weiss, C. H. *Evaluation: Methods for Studying Programs and Policies.* (2d ed.) Englewood Cliffs, N.J.: Prentice Hall, 1998.

*TRACY A. HUEBNER is coordinator for comprehensive school reform at WestEd.*

*The usefulness of program theory for monitoring and evaluation can be enhanced by incorporating information about the context in which the program operates, by defining success criteria and comparisons for judging and interpreting performance information, and by identifying sources of performance information.*

# Developing and Using a Program Theory Matrix for Program Evaluation and Performance Monitoring

*Sue C. Funnell*

Inadequacies of performance information systems, including those used for program evaluations, have been well documented (Perrin, 1998; Winston, 1999). Sometimes these inadequacies arise from incomplete program theories or simplistic applications of program theory that overlook fundamental evaluation principles. One deficiency concerns incomplete or inappropriately focused information systems. This can occur for several reasons. First, a performance information system may concentrate on inputs, processes, and activities that apply to the lowest levels of outcomes and may overlook those that are used by the program to achieve higher levels of outcomes. Second, a performance information system may focus too much on inputs, processes, and outputs and too little on outcomes. Third, there is often a failure to link performance information to explicit and defensible evaluative criteria and to some basis for interpreting and judging performance. Finally, program theory that only looks at the impact of the program and ignores other causal factors can encourage implicit and uncritical attribution of outcomes to the program.

The *program theory matrix* approach has been developed in order to provide a means of systematically addressing these concerns.[1] It is an adjunct to other approaches to the use of program theory for performance measurement and evaluation. The approach has been refined through application to many different types of programs over more than fifteen years. It is particularly useful in helping people who might be less familiar with key evaluation principles, such as those identified previously, or who are uncertain about how to apply those principles in conjunction with program theory. This chapter outlines the essential features of the approach and discusses how it has been used to address the concerns just identified.

The principles encapsulated in the program theory matrix were originally developed in 1985 as an initiative of one state government, New South Wales (Lenne and Cleland, 1987). The Australian government later recommended the application of these principles as an important part of planning evaluations of federal programs (Australian Department of Finance, 1994). The approach has been used by municipal, state, and federal government agencies and by not-for-profit agencies across a wide range of programs. For example, at the 1990 Conference of the Australasian Evaluation Society, twelve groups of authors presented papers showing adaptations and applications of the approach to the evaluation and performance monitoring of a range of different programs—management information systems, health promotion, a public information service, a trade waste program of a water utility, a tourism media campaign, a drug and alcohol program, a sports drug agency program, a state library program, a government information service marketing program, business and strategic planning in a utility, a range of HIV-AIDS programs, and a residential care program. An overview paper described the methodology and identified lessons learned concerning the methodology, drawing on the twelve papers (Funnell, 1990).

## Essential Features of the Program Theory Matrix Approach

A *program theory* as described in this chapter consists of seven components that are typically portrayed in matrix form. The program theory matrix approach begins with the articulation of a sequenced hierarchy of intended outcomes. The hierarchy commences with immediate outcomes (for example, the target group is successfully reached by the program). These are followed by a chain of intermediate outcomes (for example, changes in knowledge and practices of target group) that in turn are followed by wider and often long-term impacts (for example, alleviation or satisfaction of need that gave rise to the program). Then for each identified outcome, a series of questions is posed, the answers to which are recorded in the matrix: What would success look like (for example, the nature of the desired changes in knowledge and with whom)? What are the factors that influence the achievement of each outcome? Which of these can be influenced by the program (for example, quality of service delivery)? Which factors are outside the direct influence of the program (for example, economic climate, past experiences of clients, competing programs)? What is the program currently doing to address these factors in order to bring about this outcome (for example, staff training, risk management)? What performance information should we collect (quantitative and qualitative indicators and comparisons)? How can we gather this information (for example, interviews, observations, administrative records)? These questions, although clear and easily understood, address complex evaluative issues, such as deciding on evaluative criteria,

**Figure 9.1.  Hierarchy of Intended Outcomes for Small Businesses
Pollution Program**

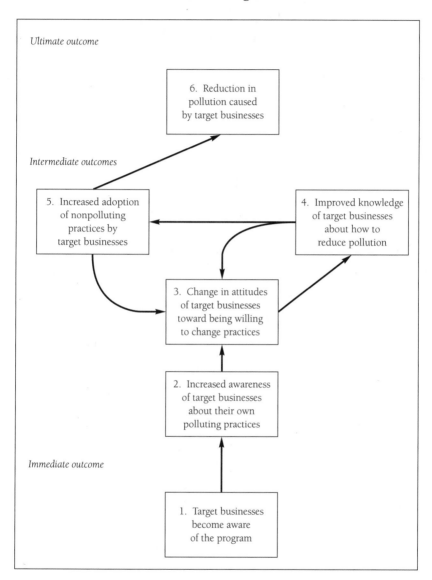

identifying potential data sources, and recognizing the impact of factors outside the program.

The hierarchy of outcomes used for the evaluation of an advisory program to change the polluting practices of small businesses is shown in Figure 9.1, which should be read from the bottom up. Table 9.1 shows the

**Table 9.1. Examples of Application of Program Theory Matrix to One Level of the Outcomes Hierarchy for the Small Businesses Pollution Program**

| 1. Intended Outcome[a] | 2. Success Criteria[b] | 3. Program Factors Affecting Success | 4. Nonprogram Factors Affecting Success | 5. Activities and Resources of Program | 6. Performance Information—Examples for Columns 2 to 5[c] | 7. Sources of Data |
|---|---|---|---|---|---|---|
| Change in attitudes of target businesses toward being willing to change practices | Agreement by businesses to meetings with program advisers with a view to identifying possible solutions; few refusals<br><br>Preparation of action plans that include defined key elements<br><br>Business-specific examples of increased willingness | Availability of confidential credible advisory assistance<br><br>Extent to which program can convince businesses of benefits of change<br><br>Extent to which the program processes are burdensome for businesses<br><br>Success with which the program engenders industry association support | Extent of target businesses' "illegal" polluting practices and whether businesses are prepared to take the risk of exposing their problems to the program in order to receive assistance<br><br>Businesses' beliefs and past experiences concerning cost and benefits of change<br><br>Whether the views and actions of competing businesses favor reducing pollution<br><br>Size and nature of businesses and capacity to com- | Promotes advisors and makes commitments about confidentiality<br><br>Identifies and promotes proven benefits to similar businesses—uses case examples<br><br>Offers and undertakes follow-up advisory visits<br><br>Develops partnerships with industry associations<br><br>Tailors paperwork and expectations to the type of business involved | Percentage of businesses that request and receive advisory assistance (columns 2 and 5), compared with targets set for each industry<br><br>Percentage of businesses receiving advice that rate the advice as credible and useful (columns 3 and 5) compared across target industries, and whether there is any relationship between perceived usefulness and apparent impact on willingness<br><br>Percentage of businesses that prepare action plans within the time frame of the program, compared | Administrative records of requests for assistance and receipt of assistance<br><br>Review of educational materials and strategies developed for the program and for each industry<br><br>Post-program anonymous survey of businesses<br><br>Advisors' client records<br><br>Interviews with advisors<br><br>Anonymous survey of businesses<br><br>Site visits and case studies by evaluator<br><br>Structured records of observations, |

mit resources to preparation of plans

Whether the offer of assistance comes at the "right time"

with target and planning guidelines (column 2)

Percentage of businesses that cite the advisory program as having contributed to willingness (column 2 and 3)

Examples of impact on willingness (column 2)

Reasons for nonparticipation or nonpreparation of plan and extent to which reasons relate to program factors and activities (columns 3 and 5) or nonprogram factors (column 4)

Extent to which successful partnerships are developed with the industry associations (columns 2 and 5)

and so forth, kept by advisors

Anonymous survey of businesses

Interviews with advisors

Interviews with advisors and with key informants in industry associations

Review of actions taken by industry associations

[a]Level 3 in Figure 9.1.
[b]Targets differ for different industries.
[c]Including comparisons.

development of the matrix for one level of outcome in this hierarchy. Many outcomes hierarchies have feedback loops and branches, and the matrix approach is as applicable to such hierarchies as it is to a simple linear one. Figure 9.1 shows some simple feedback loops.

This chapter explains the use of the matrix. However, understanding the principles underpinning the program theory matrix is more important than filling in the boxes. Moreover the columns of the matrix can be adapted to suit purpose, audience, and program context. For example, if it is useful to do so, one can split the activities and resources column into separate columns.

In addition, the underlying principles are applicable to many projects undertaken by evaluators. For example, the principles of the program theory matrix were used to develop criteria for a commissioned review of the quality of performance information in the annual performance reports of all federal government portfolios to Parliament (Funnell, 1993).

## Common Difficulties Associated with Performance Indicators and Performance Monitoring

Four common difficulties with performance indicators have been identified in the earlier discussion. In the following section, I discuss how the program theory matrix and the principles underpinning the matrix can help overcome those difficulties.

**Insufficient Attention to the Measurement of Inputs, Processes, and Outputs Needed to Achieve the Higher Levels of the Outcomes Hierarchy.** Typical inputs-processes-outputs-outcomes approaches to program theory (for example, Bennett, 1979; Suchman, 1967; Wholey, 1983), although incorporating the type of outcomes hierarchy shown in column 1 of Table 9.1, can as a consequence of their linear nature lead to dissociation between particular activities and the particular outcomes they are intended to achieve. By contrast, the program theory approach that uses a matrix (as portrayed in Table 9.1) rather than a line emphasizes that inputs (resources) and processes (activities) operate at all or most levels of the outcomes hierarchy. This approach encourages reflection on and measurement of the relationships among inputs, processes, outputs, and outcomes at all levels of the hierarchy. For example, in the small businesses pollution program, one set of inputs, processes, and outputs was applied to the lower-level intended outcome concerning change in target group awareness, and a different set of inputs, processes, and outputs was applied to a higher-level intended outcome concerning change in target group practice. Performance measures were developed for program processes at all levels of the hierarchy as a means of measuring program implementation.

This approach also reinforces the fact that lower-level outcomes do not in themselves lead to higher-level outcomes. Rather, the cause-effect process within the chain of outcomes is typically mediated by additional inputs, processes, and outputs at each level of the chain.

**Measuring What Is Easy Rather Than What Is Important: Insufficient Attention to Outcomes.** A common problem associated with the selection of performance indicators is that the indicators may relate only to what is easy to measure (typically inputs, processes, and outputs), leaving out other important aspects of performance, especially outcomes. The matrix approach makes the hierarchy of intended outcomes the backbone of the program theory to which other parts of the program theory (for example, inputs, processes, and outputs) are attached. This extra prominence of the hierarchy of outcomes can help ensure that important intermediate outcomes are not overlooked. Evaluators using the matrix are encouraged, for each outcome in the hierarchy, to make a judicious selection of measures relating to each of columns 2 to 5 in the matrix and to the relationships among them.

The outcomes hierarchy can also provide a structure for reporting the findings of an evaluation. Each chapter in the report can address one level of the outcomes hierarchy and can also include relevant information about program implementation and nonprogram factors that affect achievement of the outcome. This is an alternative to an evaluation report whose chapters are structured around methods of data collection. Examples of the use of the program theory matrix to structure an evaluation report include the evaluation of the small businesses pollution program illustrated in Figure 9.1 and Table 9.1 (Funnell and Ford, 1998) and an evaluation of a United Nations AIDS program (Funnell, 1999).

Sometimes insufficient attention to the measurement of outcomes occurs because at the time of developing the program theory, little thought is given to how outcomes might be measured. Ideally, such thought is applied early in the development of a program so that measures of outcomes can, where possible, be incorporated in routine data collections. The program theory matrix encourages the identification of sources and methods of data collection for each item of required performance information (see column 7 in Table 9.1). The identification of sources of information, although not an essential part of program theory, is the bridge between the program theory and the performance-monitoring system or evaluation design.

**Failure to Link Performance Indicators to Explicit and Defensible Evaluative Criteria and Standards.** Failure to explicate, for each intended outcome, the success criteria by which performance can be evaluated can foster measurement of the easily measurable. Explicating criteria is a step toward safeguarding against the slide to the easily measurable and the possibility of goal displacement. Being explicit about criteria draws attention to the fact that where it is not feasible to collect information about some criteria (typically qualitative criteria) through routine monitoring, then a more in-depth program evaluation may be required from time to time.

Those who apply more traditional approaches to program theory will at some point need to identify the success criteria by which the achievement of the various components of the program theory will be assessed. The program theory matrix simply provides a systematic process for undertaking and recording this step. Many traditional approaches to identifying success criteria, such as stakeholder analysis and consultation and review of relevant literature, can be used in conjunction with the matrix. For example, the development of criteria for evaluating the utilization and impacts of several program evaluations conducted by a state government agency drew on the literature on utilization of program evaluation (Funnell and Harrison, 1993). Generic program theories, such as those developed by the author and colleagues (Funnell and Lenne, 1990), are another means of gaining a rapid point of entry for identifying evaluation criteria for programs that are manifestly different but appear to have similar underlying structures.

Column 2 in Table 9.1 shows how the matrix approach to program theory encourages explication of criteria. In this example, the success criteria show how the program management and staff would like to see the broad intermediate outcome—willingness to take action—manifested in the behavior of businesses with which the program is working. In another example, the program theory developed for an evaluation of an employment program for mature-age people specified that one of its outcomes should be that participants retain jobs obtained through the program. To make this outcome measurable in a way that reflected the program intent, it was necessary to define the terms of this outcome statement. Specifications included that people placed by the program should, ideally, be in the same or a different job for twelve months or more, that the employment should be continuous, that it should be full-time permanent rather than casual, and that the results should be equitably distributed across various specified subgroups. These criteria were derived from literature on employment programs and long-term chances of success, program financial break-even information, and policy statements concerning priorities for different subgroups. The specification of these criteria was the bridge to the selection of performance indicators both for performance-monitoring purposes and for a discrete program evaluation (Funnell and Mograby, 1995). The performance information in relation to this outcome also included levels of performance that were less than the ideal—for example, employed for six months or three months, employed on a noncontinuous or casual basis. In this way, it is possible to use the step of identifying success criteria (column 2 in the matrix) to set up a goal attainment scale from "least desirable" to "most desirable" performance against each outcome.

Many data are collected that never become information because nobody ever thought very seriously about how the data might be used to draw conclusions. The program theory approach shown in Table 9.1 (see column 6) encourages program managers and evaluators to make explicit the comparisons that they will use to make judgments about the adequacy of performance or to draw cause-effect conclusions about performance. Typically, comparisons are with standards, targets, norms, past performance, and sometimes with other programs. It is important that there is some reasonable basis for select-ing standards and targets (Funnell, 1993). Examples of comparisons used for the employment program for older people were comparisons of outcomes for different subgroups to determine whether results were equitable and compar-isons with the employment rates of similar groups in the wider population. In the case of the small businesses pollution program that involved twelve very different types of industries (for example, automotive repairs, marinas, shop-ping centers, chemical industries, market gardeners), the specific criteria and targets differed depending on the size, nature, complexity, and current pollut-ing practices of each target industry.

**Uncritical Attribution of Outcomes to the Program.** The program theory matrix approach tackles the issue of causal attribution by identify-ing the possible effects both of program factors (column 3) and of external factors (column 4) on intended outcomes of the program and by encourag-ing measurement of both types of factors. By so doing, this approach explic-itly incorporates what Lipsey (1993) has referred to as the *exogenous factors* that should be included in a program theory. It is also important to identify and measure the way in which program activities (column 5) are being implemented to influence or manage those factors. A performance infor-mation system or evaluation that wishes to draw causal conclusions will need therefore to have information from each of columns 2 to 5 in Table 9.1 and about the relationships among them. In addition, prior to performance measurement and empirical evaluation, an assessment of the internal logic of the program can be undertaken, which focuses on the degree of corre-spondence among the various columns and the completeness of each. One such assessment for the small businesses pollution program would be whether the program incorporates actions to allay concerns of businesses about having their polluting practices exposed. This question can be asked independently of the further question of whether those actions are effective.

Performance information relating to causality can be drawn from a range of evaluation designs—experimental, quasi-experimental, or even nonexperimental. However, all designs typically depend on there being some identification of the program factors (in classic terms, the indepen-dent variables) and nonprogram factors (confounding variables) that are likely to affect the outcomes (dependent variables). The program logic matrix provides a framework for drawing out the most important factors in a systematic way. For example, the evaluation of the previously mentioned employment program used some quasi-experimental comparisons that were incorporated in column 6 of the matrix for that program. It compared out-comes for program participants with those of the relevant population. It made comparisons with past studies, taking account of the economic cli-mate at the time (an external nonprogram factor). And it made comparisons that suggested it was unlikely that the program was achieving its success through *creaming*—selecting only those potential participants who were most likely to succeed.

Identification of factors likely to affect results and the likely relative impact of program versus nonprogram factors positions the evaluator to make an educated judgment about how far up the outcomes hierarchy it would be sensible to attribute impacts to the program. When the nonprogram factors substantially outweigh the program factors that affect an outcome, then caution must be exercised when attributing a particular outcome to a program.

## Other Uses of the Program Theory Matrix

This chapter has focused on the use of the program theory matrix for purposes of performance measurement and evaluation and has touched on its use for assessing the internal logic of a program and for communicating findings. However, there are many other uses of program theory matrices, including using them to negotiate accountabilities and using them for team building and staff morale. As the manager of a drug and alcohol program for prisoners who was using program logic to provide a framework for developing and testing her intervention model said, "Participation in the process reassured staff that they are part of a program which has a commonsense, coherent and believable rationale. This reassurance provides a buffer against external criticism. . . . However, our evaluation process is not simply about giving a warm inner glow to staff. By exposing the assumptions underlying the program, and making them testable, we have raised expectations that they will be tested and will continue to be tested from time to time. We certainly have a commitment to doing so" (Matthews and Funnell, 1987, p. 7).

## Conclusion

The program logic matrix offers a systematic process for developing and applying program theory in a way that guards against some of the problems that commonly bedevil performance measurement systems and provides a constructive approach to designing program evaluations. It does this, first, by encouraging the development of a comprehensive approach to measurement and evaluation that gives balanced attention to inputs, processes, and outcomes. Second, it draws attention away from what is easy to measure and toward what is important to measure and encourages early consideration of the means by which all important types of information will be obtained. Third, it explicitly incorporates evaluative criteria and comparisons. Finally, it provides a systematic basis for exploring causal attribution by making provision for the identification and measurement of effects of both program factors and external factors on intended outcomes of the program.

## Note

1. The approach has usually been referred to as *program logic matrix.*

## References

Australian Department of Finance. *Doing Evaluations: A Practical Guide.* Canberra: Australian Government Publishing Service, 1994.

Bennett, C. F. *Analyzing Impacts of Extension Programs.* Washington D.C.: U.S. Department of Agriculture, 1979.

Funnell, S. "Developments in the New South Wales Approach to Analysing Program Logic." *Proceedings of the Annual Conference of the Australasian Evaluation Society,* 1990, 2, 247–256.

Funnell, S. "Reporting the Performance of Public Sector Programs." *Evaluation Journal of Australasia,* 1993, 5(2), 16–37.

Funnell, S. "An Evaluation of the United Nations Best Practices Collection: Its Strengths and Weaknesses, Accessibility, Use and Impact." Unpublished report commissioned by United Nations AIDS, Geneva, 1999.

Funnell, S., and Ford, C. "An Evaluation of Solutions to Pollution: The Small Business and Local Government Environmental Management Program of the New South Wales Environment Protection Authority." *Proceedings of the Annual Conference of the Australasian Evaluation Society,* 1998, 2, 391–412.

Funnell, S., and Harrison, C. "Utility Is in the Eye of the User." *Proceedings of the Annual Conference of the Australasian Evaluation Society,* 1993, pp. 265–292.

Funnell, S., and Lenne, B. "Clarifying Program Objectives for Program Evaluation." *Program Evaluation Bulletin 1990,* no 1. Sydney: Program Evaluation Unit of New South Wales Premier's Department, 1990.

Funnell, S., and Mograby, A. "Evaluating Employment Programs Delivered by Community Organisations." *Proceedings of the Annual Conference of the Australasian Evaluation Society,* 1995, 2, 531–552.

Lenne, B., and Cleland, H. "Describing Program Logic." *Program Evaluation Bulletin 1987,* no. 2. Sydney: Public Service Board of New South Wales, 1987.

Lipsey, M. "Theory as Method: Small Theories of Treatments." In L. Sechrest and A. Scott (eds.), *Understanding Causes and Generalizing About Them.* New Directions for Program Evaluation, no. 57. San Francisco: Jossey-Bass, 1993.

Matthews, A., and Funnell, S. "Evaluability Assessment of Drug and Alcohol Programs for Prisoners in New South Wales." Paper presented at the annual conference of the Australasian Evaluation Society, Canberra, July 1987.

Perrin, B. "Effective Use and Misuse of Performance Measurement." *American Journal of Evaluation,* 1998, 19(2), 367–379.

Suchman, E. A. *Evaluative Research: Principles and Practice in Public Service and Social Action Programs.* New York: Russell Sage Foundation, 1967.

Wholey, J. S. *Evaluation and Effective Public Management.* New York: Little, Brown, 1983.

Winston, J. A. "Performance Indicators—Promises Unmet: A Response to Perrin." *American Journal of Evaluation,* 1999, 20(1), 95–99.

*SUE C. FUNNELL is director of Performance Improvement, an Australian consultancy company specializing in program planning and evaluation and is immediate past president of the Australasian Evaluation Society.*

# 10

*The author summarizes the issues and concerns raised by the volume and discusses other recent developments for evaluators using program theory.*

# Summing Up Program Theory

*Leonard Bickman*

In this last chapter, I summarize what I think are the most interesting aspects of the previous chapters, and then I evaluate what we have learned about program theory from these and other efforts. In 1987, I edited the first volume of *New Directions for Program Evaluation* (Bickman, 1987), which dealt with program theory. I was among a small group of evaluators that year who seemed to simultaneously "discover" the need to describe better the underpinnings of the programs that we were evaluating. I was disappointed in the widespread use of black box evaluations and thought that a *New Directions for Program Evaluation* would be a good way to sensitize evaluators to this new approach to program evaluation. In 1990, I edited another volume of *New Directions for Program Evaluation* focusing on advances in program theory (Bickman, 1990). The first volume dealt with the functions of program theory, its relationship to program philosophy, its use to improve programs, its link to program implementation, and its relationship to evaluability assessment and how it could guide social change. In the second volume, the topics included conceptual issues such as how to construct program theory, the use of path analysis and tests of program theory and applications to program quality, program classification, and social science theory. Has program theory advanced in the thirteen years since that first publication? What have been the forces that have either inhibited or advanced this concept? What have the authors of the current volume contributed to our thinking about program theory? Let us start with the last question by examining the contributions of each of the chapters.

## Overview of Program Theory

The editors present an excellent overview of program theory in their introduction. They review the early history of the concept and point to the pioneering efforts by Suchman (1967) to popularize program theory. There is an informative discussion of the related and overlapping concepts of program theory, including theory-driven and theory-based evaluations. The authors then tie in the broader concept of program theory to the specifics of logic models, which are often used to operationalize program theory. The editors also describe the choices that evaluators face in developing the logic model, such as who should do it and how should input from stakeholders be obtained. They then relate the early conceptualization of theory to a two-step causal model, which clarifies some of the earlier confusions about the function of logic models. There is then a discussion of the problem of how program theory is related to causal attribution. The editors consider the demonstrated and potential benefits of program theory, followed by a discussion of the established and potential risks of using program theory, including a discussion of the concept's misuse. The latter will be highlighted in the remainder of this chapter as it relates to each author's contribution.

## Which Links Should Be Evaluated, and Which Theories Should be Used?

Weiss (Chapter Four), who encouraged the volume's editors to delve into the nature of program theory as part of a postdoctoral experience, focuses on a significant decision that evaluators must make when explicating theories. She raises the question about which links in the theory should be evaluated. Focus on the links between activities and outcomes is a major thrust of program theory. Weiss points out that the problem with most social service and educational interventions is that their efficacy is not firmly established—that is, we do not have good evidence, even in the laboratory, that the intervention is effective. Evidence for the efficacy of certain interventions in the medical and health care arena does exist. For example, if we were evaluating vaccinations already shown to be effective in clinical trials, the evaluator's job would focus only on the implementation of the vaccination program. We would want only to document that the right population was vaccinated with a vaccine that was potent. We might want to look a bit at the training of the persons delivering the vaccine and the conditions under which it was stored, but we would not need to evaluate what happens to a person's immune system once the vaccine is injected.

Our evaluations need to include events and activities, as Weiss calls them, outside the organization. A job-training program can fail, even if well implemented, if it does not lead to employment. Program theory can help us track the linkages from a program's activities to the expected outcomes. But this is a difficult task because it requires additional resources. There is therefore a need to educate and persuade funders that providing the additional resources needed for a theory-based evaluation is worth it. What is needed to make this argument more persuasive is evidence that evaluations that include program theory do result in a more informed use of the results.

But as Weiss asks, which among many potential theories do we use to find and examine the linkages from program activity to outcome? Weiss has several suggestions, including starting with program staff, administrators, and designers. But as she notes, there may not be a consensus on these linkages. In that case, she suggests the use of multiple theories. Although this alternative is a sensible one, it again requires more resources. Assuming that additional resources are not available, then trade-offs need to be made. Which should it be? Fewer subjects, fewer data points in a longitudinal study, or more theory? No easy answer here, especially one without context.

## The Importance of Causality

Struggling further with the problem of ascribing causality of any changes to the program, Davidson (Chapter Two) suggests several approaches, especially qualitative approaches. She logically argues that there is no way to eliminate all possible alternative explanations for an effect and suggests that the standard for evaluation should be similar to a legal *beyond a reasonable doubt*. Davidson introduces a five-stage method that can be used to attribute cause. First, do a needs assessment to determine level of certainty. Second, detect all the important outcomes using a goal-free perspective. Third, trace the causes and outcomes detected in stage two, again following a "theory-free" inductive approach. Fourth, add additional theories that are relevant. Finally, test the model qualitatively and quantitatively. This inductive approach is an innovative way of approaching the use of program theory. The problem I have with it is that it removes the putative strengths of the theory's approach. For example, one of the advantages of theory is that it helps identify relevant outcomes and mediators. Not to use the theory in stage two may result in missing important outcomes that are left unmeasured and thereby not even considered in stage three. Although the theory approach is not necessarily driven by the goals of the program, it should consider them. Finally, stage five is where we need the most work. As discussed more fully in Cook's chapter (Three), we do not have good methods that we can use to test program theories. But Davidson is correct when she says that context helps determine the type and extent of evidence that is needed to convince others that the program was the cause of the outcomes. Telling, or—said in a less positive way—spinning, a good story about the program and the outcomes is often what makes the difference in use of evaluations. Here, *best* means most believable or credible as seen by the audience. I think a coherent and cogent theory with the data to support it makes a stronger story than one without such information.

This volume stresses that program theory is intimately linked to concerns about causality. Although there are program models that only depict the operational relationships among program components, most theories try to explain the causal connection between the program and its intended effects. It is appropriate therefore that Rogers (Chapter Five) devote her chapter to a clarification of what is meant by causality. It is more complex and multifaceted than most think. Rogers first points out that the simple causal chain from program activities to outcomes is usually a gross over-simplification of reality, one that can have dire consequences for the program and the evaluation if this linkage is not viable (assuming that a direct connection will invariably result in overestimating the effectiveness of the program). From a theory point of view, this one-step model also will not provide information concerning why the effects were not found. Rogers notes that there are several causal relationships that are possible, including complementary causes, wherein other, sometimes conflicting, paths are possible in the same program. It is also possible that the relationship between the cause and effect is not linear and is even discontinuous, so that the level of the cause has to reach some threshold before it will produce an effect. Rogers also stresses that clients are not necessarily passive objects but take an active role in determining how programs cause effects. She discusses several other intriguing causal relationships that are possible and that can result in problems for the evaluator if not understood. Rogers's chapter can serve as a guide to what future developments are necessary if program theory is going to truly advance evaluation practice.

One of the problems with many models is their unidirectional nature. Feedback loops are not often included in the program logic. There are several reasons for this, the main one being an attempt at simplifying what can be tested. Rogers alerts us to another problem that complicates the matter even more: if feedback is delayed, then its effect may be to produce highly variable behavior. Rogers notes how difficult it is to adjust the temperature on a shower when there is a delay of even a second or so in the change of the water. In most social and educational programs, feedback may take days or weeks. This is a condition that does not lead to optimal performance and may even help produce worse performance than having no feedback. It should be clear that the causal connection is critical in program theory and that the correct specification is important. However, that specification often depends on our knowledge of the problem, which is often lacking. Another persistent theme of many of the chapters is the awareness that the validity of the program theory depends on the substantive knowledge of the field.

## The Need for Precision in Program Theory

Cook (Chapter Three) takes up a theme that runs through many of the chapters, the difficulty of attributing causality to the program. Some of the other authors in this *New Directions* issue imply or state that any evaluation design might suffice in drawing casual connections if there is a strong program theory. So to some, program theory can substitute for an experimental design. Cook contends that one of the reasons for this position is the frequent finding of ineffective community and school programs. It is easier to blame the supposedly insensitive designs used by evaluators than to confront the possibility that the results were valid and the program was ineffective. Cook provides seven reasons supporting his doubts that program theory can substitute for an experimental design. Other authors in this volume have addressed some of these reasons, but in this summary chapter they deserve to be revisited.

The lack of precision and explicitness of many theories needs to be addressed in the development of program theory. We now recognize that there is usually not one program theory that is possible but several. Often it is not specified which theory is being tested until after the study is finished. As a result, it is tempting to claim to test the theory that best fits the data. This "backward fitting" is fine as an exploratory device that could be confirmed by additional work, but that work rarely appears. Unfortunately, the lack of precision in most theories is a problem that originates in the substantive field of the problem that the program is seeking to alleviate and not in the evaluation. I think that the program theory approach has exposed the impoverished nature of the theories that underlie many of the interventions we study. The bases of programs are often political or poorly conceptualized. It is doubtful that even the best theory developed during the evaluation can help. Clearly, more research on the nature of the problems and the nature of interventions would help. So would some clear thinking about the assumptions underlying a program before it is launched. The evaluator using a program theory approach can identify these assumptions but cannot correct for their inadequacies.

Theories are often vague and also may not be accurate representations of the program. Cook points out that most program theories are linear, with no feedback loops. Moreover it is rare that theories include contextual factors, outside of the program. Theorists like Funnell (Chapter Nine) are attempting to address this problem by developing a more rigorous methodology for conducting theory-based evaluations. Finally, although there are significant conceptual problems in this area, one of the major limitations of providing more complex theories and logic models has been the dearth of analytical techniques, which Cook refers to as "technical difficulties." As the complexity of the models increases, it drives the demand for improved analytical techniques.

I am very familiar with the refrain that an evaluation did not show the expected effects simply because the evaluation was premature. Cook notes that theories, and I would add program advocates, rarely specify how long it should take for a program to have an effect. Hence when the results do not confirm positive expectations, the cry is heard that not enough time has passed. There are actually two variations of the timing issue. One is that the program has not had time to mature, often a legitimate concern. The second is that the process of change takes longer than has been allowed in the evaluation. I have dealt with these problems in several ways. The maturity issue can be managed by analyzing the data by when the participant entered the program. The assumption here is that those who enter the program later, when the program is more mature, should show stronger effects. This requires that recruitment take place over a long enough time period, so that the program does have time to settle down. Of course, without any a priori specification of how long it takes a program to mature, or measures of maturity, the defenders can still say there was not enough time. Another approach is to replicate the study with a mature program. This may entail finding a site that is using the program for several years and that is not a demonstration but an institutionalized program. I have used both of these approaches in the Fort Bragg and Stark County studies (Bickman, 1996; Bickman, Noser, and Summerfelt, 1999) to counter just such criticisms.

The second type of timing issue is the amount of time it takes for a program to have an effect. Again, as Cook notes, we are at the mercy of the quality of substantive information about the nature of the problem. Most of the fields in which we work do not have simple descriptive information that describes the course of the problem over time. I have been fortunate in some of my studies to design them so that they were longitudinal and followed participants from two to five years. This option may not be available to most evaluators, but it should be discussed with funders because it may affect the probability of finding an effect. If the theory is clear and precise about the timing issues, it would support the argument for a longer time frame for evaluations.

Cook notes that good measurement is critical for a good evaluation. Program theory can be a big advantage in helping the evaluator identify constructs that should be measured and make salient the critical ones that cannot be measured because the theory is too vague about the meaning of the construct or because no measurement tool exists. However, complex models will usually identify more constructs than can be measured, typically because of the cost of measurement. In addition, the lack of attention to measurement development in many fields means that good measures may not be available. However, this provides an excellent opportunity for the evaluator to engage the stakeholders in discussion about which constructs to measure and how well they should be measured. Although there is a consensus that multiple methods of measurement from multiple sources are the best, where to make trade-offs within a budget (Hedrick, Bickman, and Rog, 1993) is contextual and needs to be discussed with the stakeholders. This can both increase stakeholder involvement and help protect the credibility of the evaluator.

Cook, in describing his fifth concern, acknowledges that we do not have a way of knowing how many different models may fit the data. We do not have a way of knowing if some other variables would not work as well or better, nor do we have a way to test these hypothetical models against one another. This is not a problem unique to program theory but is true of experimental approaches as well. A randomized experiment may present a relatively unambiguous causal relationship among the variables, but we know that programs and their effects are complex constructs that can be interpreted in many different ways. The problem that Cook identifies here is similar to construct-of-cause and construct-of-effect validity issues that apply to all research and evaluation. There is no easy solution to this, other than more social science research and better measurement.

Cook is on target in noting, in the sixth problem, that an evaluation that depends only on its theory and not on an experimental design cannot rule out alternatives if there is no comparison condition. The counterfactual control group needs to exist to address this problem. Cook also dismisses those who believe that cause can be attributed from a complex pattern predicted and found in an evaluation. This approach, sometimes called modus operandi, is supported by analogy to other fields such as pathology, where the cause of death is attributed by carefully examining the evidence and eliminating alternatives. As Cook notes, this is possible when there is extensive and clear knowledge of the phenomenon, something rarely found in evaluation studies.

Finally, Cook's last objection to depending on program theory alone to establish cause is a form of Gresham's law of evaluation, in which bad evaluations drive out good ones. If funders believe that they can learn all they need to know without control groups, expensive measurement, and long time frames by just explicating the theory and studying the initial implementation, then why bother with expensive experimental designs? This is not mere speculation on Cook's part. Over twenty years ago, there was an emphasis on evaluability assessment, a front-end examination of the desirability of conducting a full-fledged evaluation. This seemed like a very sensible and prudent approach to evaluation funding, and Wholey (1987) described its relationship to program theory. However, in a comprehensive study of this approach in her doctoral dissertation, Rog (1985) found that almost none of the evaluability assessments were followed by evaluations, regardless of their findings. So Cook's concerns about the future are historically supported.

Program theory, in Cook's estimate, has much to offer program evaluation but within an experimental framework. It is not a substitute for experimental design in assessing causality, but rather a partner. We need to have as much unbiased information as possible about the causal effects of a program, *and* we need to conceptualize why and how those effects emerged or did not emerge.

A verbal label of a program is an imprecise method to communicate the nature of the program. Petrosino (Chapter Six) chapter notes that these labels often mask or obscure the actual intervention. He suggests that categorizing the program theory properly and including similar programs in a meta-analysis would be a significant advance. Following the early work of Lipsey, Petrosino suggests that evaluations that have an explicit model, test at least one mediating construct, and have a control group would be candidates for this meta-analytical approach. He believes that this approach can inform policy on what are effective approaches to social problems.

Petrosino also identifies a significant problem with many programs—*cascading effects* in which each subsequent mediating effect in a program produces smaller effects. This is a problem that I identified in the Fort Bragg study (Bickman, 1997), and it is a problem with all interventions that do not have a direct effect on the "targets" but must operate through a series of mediating variables. Simple algebra dictates that in a chain the links are multiplied to obtain the strength of the relationship. Thus if the connection between the first two variables is as strong as .50, then the relationship between the first and the third is .25. The effect of the intervention is severely weakened if there are several mediators between it and the ultimate outcome. I suggest that this is common and may be a major reason for the failure of many of our interventions. A related problem is the vagueness of most theories in understanding this problem. Consequently, the evaluator never knows, until after the data are collected, just how strong an intervention or its mediators need to be to have an effect. In Fort Bragg, there were statistically significant differences in parent involvement in care between the experimental and control conditions, but critics noted that there might not have been enough parent involvement (Friedman, 1996). This could be the case, but the same critics could not specify just how much involvement was needed to produce an effect. The only solution here is the researcher's lament: what is needed is more research. However, Petrosino indicates that more is not enough—it has to be of better quality. This is also a lament often made by researchers about other researchers' work.

The devil is in the details is the theme offered to us by Hacsi (Chapter Seven), a trained historian. If there is a major problem with the development of program theory, it is in the lack of details. Hacsi perceptively points out that the type of general and vague advice offered by Schorr (1997) and others on how to replicate a successful project is missing the details needed to ensure that replication. General advice to include such aspects as flexibility, coherence, and so on lacks operational definitions that are necessary for planners. How do we measure flexibility, and who has to have this flexibility in order for a program to be successful? Without these types of specifics, we are left with platitudes that do not guide planning and evaluation. Hacsi is optimistic that program theory can be of assistance here. By studying the specific linkages that represent the basic assumptions of the program, it may be possible to produce knowledge that will identify the critical elements of a program that need to be included in a successful replication.

## New Directions for Program Theory

Huebner (Chapter Eight) has taken the interesting empirical step of speaking to several evaluators and program participants about the theory-based evaluations in which they were involved. The evaluators reported that the program theory helped them and the participants clarify the program goals and improve cooperation between evaluators and participants, and it encouraged the participants to be more reflective of their practice. These are intriguing findings, though only based on interviews with three evaluators and a few participants, but they confirm what proponents of program theory have been claiming as advantages of that approach. This chapter represents a tentative first step of something that evaluators have not done much of—evaluate their own theories and methods.

Funnell (Chapter Nine) offers the richest and most in-depth account of how to conduct a theory-based evaluation, based on her many years of conducting such studies. She differentiates her approach to using logic models and program theory from others by focusing on seven essential features that are summarized in a program logic matrix. The matrix provides a visual guide to what to include in a theory-oriented evaluation. I will not review that material here but instead will concentrate on what she identifies as difficulties with what may be seen as a competing approach—the use of performance indicators. Performance indicators are often seen as a substitute for program evaluation. Performance indicators simply require the collection of outcome data, typically without an evaluation design and without any mediating variables, to reach a conclusion about the success of a program. This movement is the antithesis of program theory. Funnell points out that this approach usually does not measure the relationships among program components, promotes easy to measure constructs rather than valid ones, does not provide linkages to standards, and often makes uncritical assumptions attributing outcomes to the program. She presents her program logic matrix, which she calls a *program theory matrix,* as a remedy to these problems. A key is the creation of a hierarchy of outcomes, as shown in the matrix, which assists in planning an evaluation. Funnell later points out that feedback loops can be included, though they complicate the matrix. An appropriate statement here—and I do not know to whom to attribute it—is that all models are wrong, but some are more helpful than others. This view is critical in understanding the advantages and disadvantages of program theories.

In the thirteen years since the publication of the first *New Directions for Program Evaluation* issue on program theory, there has been much positive change. There are many more evaluations that include theory. I have also seen a huge increase in the number of requests for proposals and grant announcements that specify that the proposal must include a logic model and by inference a program theory. There is a topical interest group in the American Evaluation Association on program theory, and there are several books written on the topic. But much more remains to be done before program theory can deliver on its putative advantages that have been identified earlier (Bickman, 1987, 1990). The tools needed by evaluators to develop program theory need to be refined. Funnell's approach is a good example of that type of much-needed work. However, such efforts are not easy to support. We need, as a community, to reinforce such efforts. However, I feel that evaluators may be fighting a losing battle in their efforts to shore up weak programs with their introduction of program theory, regardless of the number of stakeholders involved in the development. A consistent theme of this *New Directions* volume is that the strength of program theory depends on the substantive knowledge of the field. The development of a strong program theory should be the responsibility of program planners and not evaluators. We have taken up that task because the advocates and developers have not done a satisfactory job in conceptualizing the programs. I hope that we can demonstrate the usefulness of program theory, so that planners can be motivated to provide us with sensible, coherent, and evaluable programs.

## References

Bickman, L. (ed.). *Using Program Theory in Evaluation.* New Directions for Program Evaluation, no. 33. San Francisco: Jossey-Bass, 1987.

Bickman, L. (ed.). *Advances in Program Theory.* New Directions for Program Evaluation, no. 47. San Francisco: Jossey-Bass, 1990.

Bickman, L. "The Application of Program Theory to the Evaluation of a Managed Mental Health Care System." *Evaluation and Program Planning,* 1996, *19*(2), 111–119.

Bickman, L. "Resolving Issues Raised by the Fort Bragg Evaluation: New Directions for Mental Health Services Research." *American Psychologist,* 1997, *52*(5), 562–565.

Bickman, L., Noser, K., and Summerfelt, W. T. "Long-Term Effects of a System of Care on Children and Adolescents." *Journal of Behavioral Health Services Research,* 1999, *26*(2), 185–202.

Friedman, R. M. "The Fort Bragg Study: What Can We Conclude?" *Journal of Child and Family Studies,* 1996, *5*(2), 161–168.

Hedrick, T. E., Bickman, L., and Rog, D. J. *Applied Research Design: A Practical Guide.* Thousand Oaks, Calif.: Sage, 1993.

Rog, D. J. "A Methodological Analysis of Evaluability Assessment." Unpublished doctoral dissertation, Vanderbilt University, 1985.

Schorr, L. B. *Common Purpose: Strengthening Families and Neighborhoods to Rebuild America.* New York: Anchor Books, 1997.

Suchman, E. A. *Evaluative Research: Principles and Practice in Public Service and Social Action Programs.* New York: Russell Sage Foundation, 1967.

Wholey, J. S. "Evaluability Assessment: Developing Program Theory." In L. Rickman (ed.), *Using Program Theory in Evaluation.* New Directions for Program Evaluation, no. 33. San Francisco: Jossey-Bass, 1987.

*LEONARD BICKMAN is professor of psychology, psychiatry, and public policy at Vanderbilt University.*

# INDEX

# Back Issue/Subscription Order Form

Copy or detach and send to:
**Jossey-Bass Inc., Publishers, 350 Sansome Street, San Francisco CA 94104-1342**

Call or fax toll free!
**Phone 888-378-2537 6AM-5PM PST; Fax 800-605-2665**

Back issues:     Please send me the following issues at $23 each.
                            (Important: please include series initials and issue number, such as EV77.)

1. EV _____

_____

_____

$ _____ Total for single issues

$ _____ Shipping charges (for single issues *only;* subscriptions are exempt from shipping charges): Up to $30, add $5$^{50}$ • $30$^{01}$–$50, add $6$^{50}$ $50$^{01}$–$75, add $7$^{50}$ • $75$^{01}$–$100, add $9 • $100$^{01}$–$150, add $10 Over $150, call for shipping charge.

Subscriptions     Please ❑ start    ❑ renew my subscription to *New Directions for Evaluation* for the year ___ at the following rate:

     ❑ Individual $65        ❑ Institutional $118
**NOTE:** Subscriptions are quarterly, and are for the calendar year only. Subscriptions begin with the spring issue of the year indicated above. For shipping outside the U.S., please add $25.

$ _____ Total single issues and subscriptions (CA, IN, NJ, NY and DC residents, add sales tax for single issues. NY and DC residents must include shipping charges when calculating sales tax. NY and Canadian residents only, add sales tax for subscriptions.)

❑ Payment enclosed (U.S. check or money order only.)
❑ VISA, MC, AmEx, Discover Card #_____ Exp. date_____

Signature _____ Day phone _____
❑ Bill me (U.S. institutional orders only. Purchase order required.)
Purchase order #_____

Name _____
Address _____

_____

Phone_____ E-mail _____

For more information about Jossey-Bass Publishers, visit our Web site at:
www.josseybass.com                     **PRIORITY CODE = ND1**

# Other Titles Available in the
# New Directions for Evaluation Series
*Jennifer C. Greene, Gary T. Henry*, Coeditors-in-Chief